CW00431699

Amiga for Beginners

Christian Spanik

A Data Becker Book
published by

Table of Contents

Introduction

Introduction

There are two groups of people who use computers. The first group already knows and understands computers. The second group lacks previous experience with computers. Commodore designed the Amiga for both types of computer users.

Most computer manuals aren't written with the absolute beginner in mind. That's where this book comes in. In this book you'll find ideas, tips, suggestions and more to help you learn about your Amiga.

There are three types of Amigas. The original model (Amiga 1000) is no longer manufactured by Commodore Amiga. The Amiga 500 is a self-contained unit including a disk drive, central processing unit and keyboard built into one case. The larger models are the Amiga 2000 and 3000. They have similarities to both the Amiga 500 and Amiga 1000, except that these larger models can be easily expanded for increased performance. *The Amiga for Beginners* was written specifically for Amiga 500, Amiga 2000 and Amiga 3000 owners.

This book includes programming examples as well as instructions for connecting and operating the Amiga. Programming isn't just for programmers. This book shows you the basics of simple programming for your Amiga.

Amiga for Beginners helps you understand all you need to know as an Amiga owner, and hopefully entertain you as you learn.

Christian Spanik

Editor's note: We have updated this book to include Workbench 1.3 and Workbench 2.0. The Amiga Workbench is an ever expanding and improving system. Programs are changed and added to the Workbench to upgrade and improve the Amiga operating system. Therefore the programs listed in this book may not appear in the drawers or diskettes listed. If a program does not appear in the drawer mentioned, try looking in other drawers on the Workbench and Extras diskettes for the program. We will note the differences between Workbench 1.3 and 2.0 whenever possible.

1
Starting Out

1.   Starting Out

This chapter shows you how to unpack and assemble the components of your Amiga. You'll learn what components should be in the package when you open it, how they are connected and how to switch your Amiga on and off. This chapter also describes what goes on inside the Amiga.

• Instructions appear in the book like this to indicate that you must perform this step.

Some words may appear throughout this book which you may not recognize. These new words appear in *italics* when first mentioned. We'll define these unknown words in Appendix B.

1.1   Unpacking and setup

Be very careful when you unpack the Amiga. Although the polystyrene cushions in the carton protect the Amiga from damage during shipment, they can break easily if you carelessly unpack the Amiga.

• Open the Amiga carton and remove the polystyrene cushions.

The Amiga carton contains the following:

A *central processing unit* with an internal *disk drive*

A keyboard (either separate or connected to the central processing unit). If you have an Amiga 2000, a coiled cable for connecting the keyboard to the central processing unit is also included.

A *mouse* (a small hand-held device with two buttons and a long winding cable)

At least two diskettes

A *power supply* (Amiga 500) or a *power cord* (Amiga 2000)

If you cannot find all of these items, search the box or boxes again. If you still cannot find everything, contact your dealer about the missing equipment.

Next, open the *monitor* box if you purchased a monitor (video screen). Remove the top polystyrene cushions and lift the monitor out of the box.

Assembling the Amiga

Place the Amiga on a table or desktop. You should have at least one square foot of free space around it. If you have an Amiga 2000 or 3000 (which has a small cooling fan) make sure that nothing blocks the fan outlet in the back. There are air vents in different places on the Amiga models. These air vents must be kept clear too because they help ventilate the Amiga.

For Amiga 2000 and 3000 owners only (Amiga 500 users can skip to the paragraph called *Preparing the mouse*):

• Take the keyboard cable (the coiled cable).

• Plug the free end of the keyboard cable into the keyboard connector jack (the round jack) near the front center of the Amiga 2000's central processing unit. On the Amiga 3000 the keyboard connector is located on the side and middle of the case.

- Pick up the mouse (the small box with the two buttons on top) and turn the mouse upside down.

Preparing the mouse

After turning the mouse upside down, you should see a small ball poking through a hole in the bottom. You must remove the piece of foam holding the ball in place before using the mouse.

- Press on the plastic cover holding the ball, push in the direction indicated by the arrows molded into the plastic. Push until the cover opens.

- Remove the foam and put the ball back into the mouse.

- Slide the cover on by pushing it in the direction opposite the arrows.

The mouse cable goes into a connector located on the back of the Amiga 500. The mouse connectors on the Amiga 2000 are located on near the bottom right of the front side of the central processing unit. The mouse connectors on the Amiga 3000 are located on the side of the central processing unit.

Note that there are two of these connections. The first connector on the Amiga 500 is marked with **1 JOYSTICK** and the second one is **2 JOYSTICK**. The mouse connectors on the Amiga 2000 and 3000 are not marked. Therefore, the connector closest to the keyboard connector is **1 JOYSTICK.**

- Plug the mouse into the first joystick connector (this is marked **1 JOYSTICK** on the Amiga 500; it's the one closest to the keyboard connector on the Amiga 2000 and 3000).

Make sure that you have a minimum of 6" x 6" of table space available for moving the mouse.

- Connect the monitor.

The Amiga 500 and 2000 accept three types of monitors:

Amiga 500 and 2000 monitor

1.   Commodore RGB monitor.

This monitor displays a high quality picture. It's recommended for those who seriously and regularly use the Amiga. The monitor includes a special connecting cable with plugs on each end. The wider one of these plugs connects to the Amiga's *RGB* connector. This connecter is marked **VIDEO** on the Amiga 2000 and **RGB-VIDEO** on the Amiga 500 (more about RGB later). Two small bolts on the plug fasten the cable to the Amiga once the plug is in place. The Commodore RGB monitor packaging also has a Y connector and an audio cable for the audio inputs. The Y connector plugs into the two jacks behind the Amiga marked **L-AUDIO** and **R-AUDIO**. You'll find these jacks to the right of the mouse connections (Amiga 500) or to the left of the **SERIAL PORT** connection (Amiga 2000). The audio cable plugs into the AUDIO jack in the monitor.

2.   Monochrome monitor.

The **MONO** output of the Amiga delivers a *composite* signal. This signal combines various data, such as picture information and synchronization signal, into one signal. The monochrome signal requires only one cable.

3.   A black and white or color television set.

You can use your television set but you need a modulator and an appropriate cable. See the modulator manual for connection instructions. If your television set can also function as a composite monitor, you can connect the television through the **MONO** jack on the Amiga. The disadvantage is that color televisions only run through the **MONO** jack, which displays monochrome signals.

The Amiga 3000 will also accept a VGA multi-sync monitor.

Amiga 3000
monitor

1.   VGA monitor (Amiga 3000).

This monitor displays the highest quality picture. It's recommended for those who use the Amiga professionally. The monitor includes a special connecting cable with plugs on each end. These plugs will differ depending on the brand of monitor. The plug connects to the Amiga's *VGA* connector, marked **VGA** on the Amiga 3000. Two small bolts on the plug fasten the cable to the Amiga once the plug is in place.

NOTE:

If your television has no composite video input, or if you prefer a color output, you'll need a *modulator* box. This box allows RGB video transmission through a television. Check with your dealer for availability. Also, if you bought a non-Commodore monitor, you'll need a Y cable and an audio cable for connecting your monitor to the Amiga's sound output. You can buy these at any electronics store.

Power

Computers require power to run. Your Amiga operates under normal house current:

For Amiga 500 owners:

•   Make sure that the power supply is switched to 0 (OFF).

•   Take the power supply (the box with a cable on either side).

- Plug the small square plug into the matching jack in back of your Amiga 500. Insert the other plug into an electrical outlet.

For Amiga 2000 and 3000 owners:

- Make sure the power switch on the central processing unit is switched to **0** (OFF).

- Find the gray or black power cord.

- Plug the small square end into the jack marked **POWER**.

- Plug the other end into your electrical outlet.

A properly connected Amiga 500 should look similar to the following:

Assembled Amiga 500

NOTE: You may want to purchase a *power strip* (a multiple-outlet board). These strips allow you to <u>safely</u> connect all the electrical equipment to one electrical outlet.

1.2   Amiga hardware

Before you switch the Amiga on, you should learn about all the equipment that make up the Amiga. These individual units are known as *hardware*. The *software*, or computer programs, pass instructions to the hardware.

*Central
processing
unit*

This book mentioned the *central processing unit*, or CPU, a number of times in the previous section. The CPU is the brain of the computer. This housing contains the memory chips and fundamental technology which the Amiga requires for operation. The central processing unit is either a self-contained unit with a built-in keyboard (Amiga 500) or a large box (Amiga 2000) or a streamlined case (Amiga 3000).

The Amiga uses *LEDs* (light emitting diodes) to let you know that the power is on or a disk is being accessed. The Amiga 500 LEDs are above the keyboard and beneath the *AMIGA* brand name. The red LED marked **POWER** lights up when the power is on. The green LED on the Amiga 500 marked **DRIVE** lights up only when the disk drive runs. The Amiga 2000, has two LEDs on the left and one on the right front of the central processing unit.

The red LED on the left marked **POWER** on the 2000 lights up when the power is on. The red LED on the right lights up when the disk drive is operating. The green LED marked **HARD DISK** on the Amiga 2000 lights up when the Amiga accesses a hard drive. The Amiga 3000 LEDs are located on the front of the case and operate similar to the Amiga 2000 LEDs.

*Floppy   disk
drives*

The floppy disk drive built into the Amiga allows you to store and recall programs and files. This disk drive uses 3-1/2" *floppy diskettes*. These diskettes are square plastic cases containing thin mylar magnetic disks. An aluminum gate covers the part of the actual diskette. It's only opened by the Amiga disk drive when you insert the disk. You can purchase these diskettes at any computer store.

The disk drive is located on the right side (Amiga 500) or front (Amiga 2000 and 3000) of the central processing unit.

Hard disks are similar to floppy disk drives, but are much faster and hold more information. You can install a hard disk in the Amiga 2000 and 3000 case or external models can be plugged into the Amiga 500.

Mouse

The mouse is the key to the Amiga's user-friendliness. You'll constantly use the mouse for operating the computer. Once the Amiga is running, the Amiga displays the mouse on the screen as an arrow pointing up and left. This arrow is called the *mouse pointer*. It moves around the screen in the direction you move the mouse on the table. You can then select certain items by using the two buttons on top of the mouse. See Chapter 2 for detailed instructions on mouse operation.

The only difference between the Amiga keyboard and a typewriter keyboard are a few extra keys. Well discuss these special keys in Chapter 2.

*Commodore
monitor*

When you look at the front of the Commodore monitor closely, you'll notice a cover running along the bottom front of the monitor. There is a small notch directly below the *AMIGA* logo or Commodore nameplate. Reach into the notch with your finger and pull down. The cover flips down and reveals the following control knobs:

*H.Position
V.Hold*

The first knob controls the horizontal position of the picture. The second knob adjusts the vertical position. These have the same function as horizontal hold and vertical hold on television sets.

Color/Tint

The next two knobs control color intensity. If you turn them, you'll discover that they easily lock into one particular position. This is the central position.

Bright/Cont

The next two knobs control picture brightness and contrast. These have locking central positions like the **Color** and **Tint** knobs.

Volume

The next knob adjusts the volume. It doesn't have a central position because you'll notice immediately if it's set too high or too low.

Video Mode

This switch has three positions: **RGB**, **SEP** and **COMPOSITE**. The RGB position is the normal setting.

1.3   Interfaces and expansion

This section describes the remaining hardware *interfaces* (connections) of the Amiga.

The Amiga 500 has 512K of *memory*. The Amiga 2000 and 3000 can have much more memory installed when purchased. The Amiga 500, 2000 and 3000 have connectors for later memory expansion.

You can plug *joysticks* and *lightpens* into your Amiga through the two mouse connectors.

Expansion bus/slots

The recessed connector on the left side of the Amiga 500 is called the *expansion bus*. The Amiga 2000 CPU contains both IBM-PC compatible and Amiga *expansion slots*. The Amiga expansion bus is known as the Zorro II bus. The Amiga 3000 CPU contains Zorro III expansion slots which is an improved Zorro II bus. Any hardware expansion which you may add later, such as memory expansion or hard disks, will plug into the expansion bus/slots.

*   Turn the Amiga around if you can, so you can see the remaining hardware interfaces.

Parallel port

You're already familiar with the **RGB** connector, power connector, **MONO** connector and audio connectors. The *Parallel port*, or *Centronics interface*, is used mainly for printer interfacing. You can easily connect your Amiga to other equipment called *peripherals*. The most common example of a peripheral is a printer. The Centronics interface allows you to connect your Amiga to many different types of printers.

All the information you need to connect the Amiga to a printer is stored on the diskettes that were included with your Amiga. This information is called *printer drivers*. The printer drivers for the Amiga support three color printers as well as a number of black-and-white printers. A few of these printers are: Alphapro 101, Brother HR-15XL, CBM MPS-1000, Diabolo 630, Diabolo Advantage D25, Diabolo C-150, Epson FX/RX series, Epson JX-80, HP LaserJet, HP LaserJet Plus, Okidata 292, Okidata 92, Okimate 20 and Qume Letterpro 20. A generic printer setting also exists.

NOTE:

If your printer isn't on the above list, try the Epson printer driver before you try any other printer driver (see Section 2.10 [Preferences] for more information). Since many companies consider Epson the standard printer configuration, most printers are Epson compatible. If you haven't purchased a printer yet, ask your dealer if he knows whether the Amiga has a printer driver for the printer you plan to buy. You can also ask your dealer whether the printer will work with the generic driver.

CAUTION:

Before you connect any printer or use any printer cable, first talk to your dealer. Some *pins* (the little metal prongs inside the plug) carry up to 5 volts of electrical current. One wrong connection could seriously damage your Amiga.

Also, be sure to buy a printer cable specifically for your Amiga (a cable for Amiga 500, Amiga 2000 or Amiga 3000, etc.). The best thing to do is tell your dealer you want a printer cable for your Amiga model and not just for an Amiga. Most IBM printer cables will work with the Amiga 500, 2000 and 3000, but NOT with the early Amiga 1000. Make sure to get the right printer cable.

Disk drive

The *Disk drive* port is on the right of the audio connectors on the Amiga 500, on the left on the Amiga 2000, and below the cooling fan on the Amiga 3000. This port accepts an external Amiga floppy disk drive.

Serial port

The *Serial port* is used to connect a *modem* to the Amiga. Modems (abbreviation for modulator/demodulator) allow you to exchange computer data by telephone lines. Some printers also use the serial connector. The serial port can also be used to connect other computers or terminals to your Amiga.

1.4   Booting The Amiga

If you connected everything according to the descriptions in the first section, you're ready to switch on, or *boot up*, the Amiga.

- Switch on the monitor (see your monitor manual for instructions).

- Switch on the Amiga. The Amiga 500 power switch is on the power supply, the Amiga 2000 switch is on the rear of the central processing unit, the Amiga 3000 switch is on the front of the central processing unit.

You'll notice that the screen blinks and changes color. This is normal. The Amiga performs a *self-test* (checks itself out to see that everything is in working order). Eventually a picture appears on the screen—a hand holding a diskette or a similar picture requesting a WorkBench or Kickstart diskette. The Amiga 1000 model needed this Kickstart diskette to supply it with some basic operating information.

NOTE:

The Amiga 500, 2000 and 3000 have this Kickstart information built into the computer, so it doesn't need this diskette. Whenever you see a reference like "insert the Kickstart diskette", here or in any other book, ignore it and go to the next set of instructions.

Amiga 1000

For Amiga 1000 owners only:

- Take your Kickstart diskette, making sure that the label is up and the metal part of the diskette faces the drive.

- Push it gently in the disk drive.

A picture appears on the screen—a hand holding a diskette named Workbench or a similar picture requesting the Workbench diskette.

- When the drive stops, press the button underneath the disk drive slot. The Amiga will eject the diskette about halfway out of the disk drive.

- Remove the partially ejected Kickstart diskette.

Floppy disk
Amiga owners

For all Amiga owners who don't have a hard disk installed in their Amiga System:

- Insert the Workbench diskette. The Amiga automatically loads the Workbench from this diskette.

*Hard disk
drive owners*

Amiga owners that have a hard disk drive installed in their system will not see the picture requesting the Workbench diskette. Amigas with hard disk drives will usually automatically load the Workbench from the hard disk. This process is called *auto-booting*.

NOTE:

NEVER eject a diskette while the disk drive is in operation (the drive light is on). You'll not only lose the data stored on the diskette but you may risk extensive damage to the disk drive.

2
The
Workbench
Diskette

2. The Workbench Diskette

This chapter explains the concept of `Intuition`. It's the Amiga user interface. Along with `Intuition` are instructions for using the mouse, and the basic terms used with `Intuition`. These terms include icons, drawers, windows, pulldown menus and menu items. The main subject of this chapter, however, is the Workbench diskette because it's the diskette you'll use most often in the Amiga.

This chapter also discusses the different drawers in the Workbench diskette. You'll learn how to get information about a program, format diskettes, copy diskettes, set a clock and even change the Amiga's screen colors.

You'll also use the Amiga's utilities in this chapter. The `Clock` and `Calculator` are practical yet useful utilities.

Most important, you'll learn how to make a *backup* of your Workbench diskette. You should use the original diskettes that came with your Amiga only when absolutely necessary. Backing up diskettes gives you copies of original diskettes that you can use without worrying about possibly destroying the original data.

Workbench Versions

There are different versions of the Amiga Workbench. A specific version number designates these different versions. These versions include Workbench 1.3 and Workbench 2.0. Check the label of your Workbench diskette to make sure you are using one of these versions.

Workbench 2.0 is an upgrade from Version 1.3. It greatly enhances the performance of the Amiga. Unfortunately this upgrade requires certain hardware and memory configurations to operate on an Amiga. Some Amiga 500 and 2000 models may require hardware modifications in order to run Workbench 2.0. These hardware modifications are basically the installation of a greatly enhanced and improved custom chip set or additional memory expansion. See your dealer for possible upgrades.

Don't despair if your Amiga will not run Workbench 2.0. Workbench 1.3 is an excellent version of the Amiga operating system. All of your work can be performed using this version of the operating system.

We'll discuss both Workbench Versions 1.3 and 2.0 in this book. We'll point out the differences between the two versions so Amiga users of either version will find this book useful.

2.1   Intuition

A white border surrounding a blue screen appears when the Amiga boots for the first time. The top part of this border displays the words AmigaDOS. You'll hear the disk drive operate. Your Amiga briefly displays the following on your screen (your screen display may differ slightly):

```
Copyright © 1985, 1985 Commodore-Amiga, Inc.
All rights reserved.
Release 1.3
A500/A2000 Workbench disk. Release x.x version 34.xx
```

This is the *Startup-Sequence* which loads (or boots) the Workbench program. The x's represent the release and version numbers and may vary depending on your version of the Workbench.

Operating system

A computer is dumb and it stays dumb until a program tells it exactly what to do. This is true of any computer. One of these programs permanently resides in the Amiga memory. When you switch the Amiga on, this program tells it how to do certain basic tasks. This would include what diskette it needs next (these are the tasks handled by the Kickstart diskette in the Amiga 1000). We call this "housekeeping" program the *operating system*.

Software, or *programs*, tell the Amiga to perform a certain sequence of commands in a specific order. The first software the Amiga reads is from the Workbench diskette when booting up. As the Workbench loads, the Amiga tells time, determines whether an external disk drive is connected, computes the amount of available memory and more (see Chapter 4 for more information).

Intuition

Intuition, loaded at the same time Workbench is booting, has the most influence on your work with the Amiga. Intuition is a *user interface*. A user interface acts as the simplest form of communication between user and computer. This is important, since Intuition is part of the operating system. It displays text, windows and graphics on the screen. Intuition stays in the background as it does its work. You can open many windows at once, and perform different tasks in these windows. You can display graphics in one window, calculations in a second and text in a third, all at the same time. Like the desk in your office, Intuition lets you open drawers, page through your work, or watch the clock.

After Workbench 1.3 loads, the following message appears on the screen:

`Amiga Workbench. Version 1.x. 406400 Free Memory`

Workbench 2.0 also displays additional information about the type of memory available in your Amiga:

`410624 graphics mem  1862088 other mem`

These numbers may be different from the numbers which appear on your screen. The version number may be higher since Commodore is continually improving the operating system of the Amiga. The amount of free memory depends on memory expansion, the number of disk drives and screens currently in use.

Icons

When the Workbench finishes loading, either a screen (1.3) or a window (2.0) appears on your monitor. The word Workbench is in the top border. This top border is called the *title bar*. One of the major differences between Workbench 1.3 and Workbench 2.0 is that in Workbench 1.3 the Workbench is always a screen. Workbench 2.0 allows you to select whether the Workbench appears as window or as a screen. You can place a window on a screen but a screen cannot be placed in a window.

You'll see at least two diskette pictures on the screen. These pictures are called *icons*. `Intuition` draws the icons. These icons form the basis of the Amiga's operating system.

Each disk drive icon has a name. The name under each diskette icon describes the title of the diskette currently in that drive. One drive icon is named `Workbench x.x` and the other drive icon is named `Ram Disk`. The x represents the release number and varies depending on which version of the Workbench you're using.

If you have a hard disk drive connected to your Amiga, you may see several disk icons. Hard drives are usually divided into partitions. These partitions act as individual diskettes. This is done because hard drives can hold so much information so it is best to divide the information into manageable partitions.

The mouse pointer is also displayed on the Workbench.

2.2   Mouse control

Using a computer mouse usually requires some practice, especially if you've never used one before. This section helps you perform your first mouse input.

- Clear some space on the table or desk next to your Amiga.

- Put your right hand on the mouse so that its two buttons face up and the wire leading from the mouse to the Amiga points away from you. Your forefinger and middle finger should rest on the buttons.

- Keep the mouse in contact with the table as move it.

The pointer on the screen moves in the same direction as the mouse.

NOTE:

When you move the mouse away from you, the pointer moves up the screen; moving the mouse toward you brings the pointer down. When we tell you to move the mouse in a certain direction, move your mouse so that the pointer moves in this direction.

- Move the mouse so that the pointer moves near the center of the display.

- Press the left mouse button once.

You'll see that even moving the mouse has no effect on the screen. There is an exception to this rule:

- Move the pointer up until it rests on the title bar (the bar running across the top of the screen).

- Press and hold down the left mouse button.

- Move the pointer.

Moving the screen

If you continue to hold the left mouse button down, the entire screen moves as you move the mouse. If you move the mouse down, the screen moves down as well. If you move the entire screen down, you'll see that there is nothing behind the screen. Then everything, including the title bar and the mouse pointer, disappears below the screen.

- Move the entire screen down and release the left mouse button.

- Now try to move the pointer up above the screen.

You'll quickly discover that the mouse pointer cannot move above the title bar. As long as you move the mouse without pressing the left mouse button, the pointer cannot move up. The mouse pointer can only move inside the active screen.

- Move the pointer up until it rests on the title bar. Then press and hold the left mouse button while moving the pointer up.

The screen returns to the top of the display. You can move almost the entire working surface in this way. We'll discuss the reasons and advantages of moving screens in the next several pages.

- Move the pointer up onto the middle of the display again and press the right mouse button.

Workbench
pulldown
menu

Watch the title bar change when you press the right mouse button. Workbench 1.3 contains three menus; `Workbench`, `Disk` and `Special`. Workbench 2.0 contains four menus; `Workbench`, `Windows`, `Icons` and `Tools`. Whenever you press the right mouse button while in the Workbench, these words appear at the top border. This top border is called the *menu bar* because it lists *menu titles*.

- Press and hold the right mouse button and move the pointer up onto the word `Workbench`.

NOTE:

If you run out of room for mouse movement but the pointer still hasn't reached its target, lift the mouse off the table and place it closer to you. Now you can continue moving the pointer up.

When the tip of the pointer reaches the word `Workbench`, a set of words appear below the word. This set is a *pulldown menu*, because it pulls down like a window shade. Each word in a pulldown menu is a *menu item* or *item* for short.

- Keep holding down the right mouse button (this keeps the pulldown menu open).

- Move the pointer onto the `Workbench` menu title.

- Move the pointer up and down inside the `Workbench` menu.

You select items this way. Even when you leave the pulldown menu, the Amiga keeps the pulldown menu open until you release the right mouse button.

- Move the pointer out of the open **Workbench** menu.

- Workbench 2.0 users should move the pointer onto the word **Window**. Workbench 1.3 users should move the pointer onto the word **Disk**.

The new pulldown menu appears as soon as the pointer reaches **Window** or **Disk** (with the right mouse button pressed down). Any previously open pulldown menus automatically close.

- Keep the right mouse button depressed and move the pointer to the word **Special** if using 1.3 or **Workbench** if using 2.0

Workbench 1.3 users will see that two items in the **Special** menu Redraw and Version, appear in a darker print than the other items. Workbench 2.0 users will see that one item, Last Message, is in lighter type. The items in light type are called ghosted items.

- Move the pointer to the Version menu item.

Version behaves differently from the ghosted items in this pulldown menu. As you move the pointer over Version, notice that its letters and background colors change.

- Release the right mouse button.

Select

Select a menu item from a pulldown menu by moving the pointer to the desired item and releasing the right mouse button. The term select is used throughout this book to refer to this procedure.

A message appears in the title bar when you select Version. This message tells you which version of the Workbench diskette is currently in use. The information in the title bar may appear similar to the following:

```
Kickstart Version 33.180. Workbench Version
33.56
```

Your version of Workbench may be different. Any Workbench version higher than 33.56 will work.

Version makes it easy to distinguish between Workbench diskette releases. A higher version number usually indicates a more recent version. If you have any version less than 33.56 (33.47, for example), check with your Amiga dealer on how to obtain a copy of the latest Workbench.

Knowing the version number can be very useful when talking to your dealer or a software manufacturer about your Amiga and the version of the operating system you're currently using.

The Last Message item works in a similar way. As soon as the Amiga displays an error message on the Workbench screen, the message appears in the title bar until you press a mouse key. If you accidentally press a mouse key without reading the error message, select Last Message to redisplay the error.

Ghost items

You can select any easily read menu items. You cannot access the menu items which appear lighter on the screen. These gray menu items are called *ghost items*. A good rule to remember is: If you can read it clearly, you can select it.

You now know how to recognize and select an available menu item.

Keyboard pointer movement

You can also use the keyboard to move the pointer. Notice the two keys near the bottom of your keyboard which are on the left and right side of the (Spacebar). The (Spacebar) is the long key at the bottom of the keyboard.

The key on the left is labelled with either a C= or an A. This key has different names depending on your Amiga model. It's either called the <Commodore logo> key or the left <Amiga> key. The key on the right is labeled with an A. It's called the right <Amiga> key.

Since we do not want to confuse you, we'll use <Commodore logo> and right <Amiga> keys in this book instead of using a specific key symbol. Therefore when we tell you to press the <Commodore logo> key and you only have a left <Amiga> key, press the left <Amiga> key instead.

Note the four ← → ↓ ↑ keys between the keyboard and the numeric keypad. These arrow keys are the *cursor keys*.

• Move the pointer to the bottom edge of the display.

• Press and hold either the <Commodore logo> or right <Amiga key>, then press and hold the ↑ key.

The pointer moves straight up without you having to touch the mouse. Although the pointer moves slowly at first, it will move faster.

• Press each of the other cursor keys while holding either the <Commodore logo> key or the right <Amiga> key.

NOTE:

You can move the pointer even faster by holding the ⇧ (Shift) key. There are two ⇧ keys on the Amiga keyboard. They're located diagonally above the <Commodore logo> key and the <Amiga> key.

When the ⇧ key is pressed in combination with the cursor keys and the <Commodore logo> key or the right <Amiga> key, the cursor will jump in that direction.

You can activate the menu bar by pressing the right <Amiga> key and the right (Alt) key at the same time. Select the Redraw item from the keyboard as follows:

- Press and hold the right <Amiga> key and the (Alt) key.

- Move the pointer with the cursor keys until the pointer is on **Workbench** for 2.0 users and **Special** for 1.3 users.

- Move the pointer to Redraw All (2.0) or Redraw (1.3) with the cursor keys.

- Release the right <Amiga> key and the (Alt) key to select Redraw All or Redraw.

Because Intuition is mouse-oriented, we'll only discuss using the mouse in this book. However, you should be familiar with the keyboard method just in case your mouse develops problems. Workbench 2.0 users can also alter the keys used to move the mouse with the keyboard by using the fkey program in the Utilities drawer.

Diskette Contents

Intuition allows you to view, access and organize the data and other information contained in a diskette.

The diskette icon on the screen shows you which diskette is currently in your drive. At this point you're probably wondering, "What can I do with it besides moving it around the screen?"

As mentioned earlier, you can actually consider your Amiga as an electronic desk. You can move items around to get a better view, reorganize drawers and put extra objects away, just as you do with a real desk and office space.

Clicking icons

The act of pressing and releasing the left mouse button when the pointer is on an icon is called *clicking*. Clicking normally selects icons. Clicking the diskette icon only changes its color or appearance. This shows that the icon is active.

When we tell you to "click on the icon" we're referring to moving the pointer to that specific icon and then pressing and releasing the left mouse button.

- Move the pointer to the Workbench diskette icon. Press and release the left mouse button one time.

The diskette icon only changes color or appearance when you click on it. Even moving the pointer off the icon has no effect on it. However, the diskette icon changes back to its original appearance if you move the pointer to any part of the blue field and press the left mouse button.

- If the Workbench diskette icon is not active, move the pointer onto the Workbench diskette icon.

- Press and hold the left mouse button.

- Move the pointer and release the left mouse button.

Notice that the diskette icon is moving under the pointer. You have now selected an icon, clicked on it and moved it to another area on the screen. Using the mouse to move an icon or symbol is called *dragging*.

To place the diskette icon at a new location, release the left mouse button.

The Amiga changes the color or appearance of a selected icon. This principle applies to all Amiga icons. We'll use the term *active* to describe a selected icon or word.

- If the Workbench diskette icon is not active, move the pointer onto it and press the left mouse button.

- Workbench 2.0 users should select the Information item from the **Icons** pulldown menu. Workbench 1.3 users should select the Info item from the **Workbench** pulldown menu.

The following is an illustration of a typical Info window:

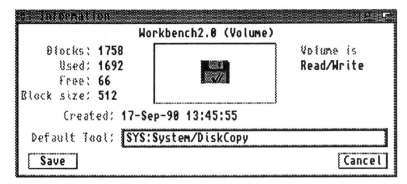

Info window

A long box appears near the top of the screen. The title bar on the top of the screen reads Information (2.0) or Info Release 1.3 (1.3).

The **Information** window displays important information about the programs and files on your diskettes. It lists information on the diskette in the disk drive. This information includes whether a file is *read-only* (you can't save data to the diskette); the amount of free storage space available on the diskette; and the date the diskette was formatted.

The type of information in the Information window depends on whether you selected a disk or a file. Before you can see what is on the Workbench, you must close the **Info** window.

- Move the mouse pointer to the small square in the upper left corner of the **Information** window. Notice the small black dot in the center of the small square.

- Click on that square with the mouse.

The small square is called a *close gadget*. Close gadgets close the currently active window when you click in them. Only a few windows do not have a close gadget. The Workbench display returns after you click on the close gadget. Click on the Workbench diskette icon once again.

- Workbench 2.0 users should select the Information item from the **Icons pulldown menu**. Workbench 1.3 users should select the Info item from the **Workbench** pulldown menu.

The **Information** window returns without any diskette activity. The Amiga remembers the information from you opening the diskette before. This requires only a small amount of memory space. The memory indicator shows exactly how much memory is available for you to use.

- Close the **Information** window again by clicking on its close gadget.

2.3   Windows

Now that you know how to open icons and the **Information** window, you can open the **Workbench** diskette window.

- If the **Workbench** diskette icon is not active, move the pointer onto it and press the left mouse button.

- **Workbench** 2.0 users should select the **Open** item from the **Icons pulldown menu**. Workbench 1.3 users should select the **Open** item from the **Workbench** pulldown menu.

Opening the Workbench diskette window

Workbench 1.3 users will see the mouse pointer change into two clouds with Zs drawn in these clouds. This pointer is the *wait pointer*. It tells you that the Amiga is performing an operation. In a few moments the wait pointer changes back into the regular mouse pointer. A window then appears on the screen.

This window contains *drawer* icons, a trash can, a shell icon and a large question mark which appears in front of a box. Your screen display may differ slightly depending on the Workbench version you are using. Workbench 1.2 did not contain the Shell and Prefs drawer. Instead Workbench 1.2 has a Preferences program and a Demos drawer. Before you look at the contents of the window, look at the window itself.

Workbench 2.0 users will see the mouse pointer change into a clock symbol as a wait pointer. Workbench 2.0 added several improvements to the previous system. These improvements include the ability to display the Workbench as a window or a screen, enhanced sizing gadgets, and more diskette usage displays. The Workbench menus have also been improved. The following diagrams show the Workbench 2.0 and Workbench 1.3 menus and displays.

Workbench 2.0 menus

Workbench	Window	Icons	Tools
Backdrop	New Drawer	Open	ResetWB
Execute Command	Open Parent	Copy	
Redraw All	Close	Rename	
Update All	Update	Information	
Last Message	Select Contents	Snapshot	
Version	Clean up	UnSnapshot	
Quit	Snapshot	Leave Out	
	Show	Put Away	
	View By		
		Delete	
		Format Disk	
		Empty Trash	

1.3 menus

Workbench	**Disk**	**Special**
Open	Empty Trash	Clean up
Close	Initialize	Last Message
Duplicate		Redraw
Rename		Snapshot
Info		Version
Discard		

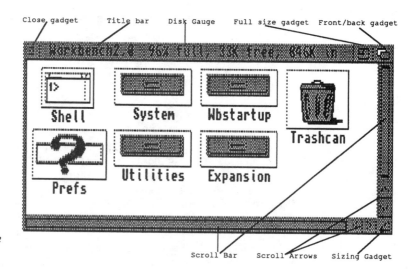

*Workbench
2.0 diskette
window*

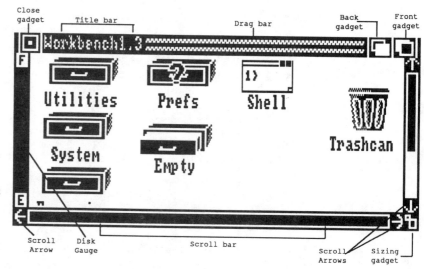

*Workbench
1.3 diskette
window*

You should recognize the close gadget in the upper left corner of the window.

• Move the pointer onto the close gadget and click on it.

The window closes and the Workbench display returns. The Workbench diskette icon returns to its original appearance. You tell the Amiga to close the window when you select the close gadget.

Double-
clicking

There's an easier and faster way to open diskettes and programs than using the Open item. Icons also open if you move your mouse pointer onto an icon and press the left mouse button twice in rapid succession. This process is called *double-clicking*.

• Move the pointer onto the Workbench diskette icon.

• Press the left mouse button twice in rapid succession (double-click). This may take some practice but it's very easy once you learn it.

This opens the **Workbench** window. At the top of this window is a close gadget and the disk name **Workbench x.x**. The x represents the number corresponding to your version of Workbench.

Multitasking

Window title bars indicate an inactive window by different colors (2.0) or by ghost print (1.3). Workbench 2.0 uses different color title bars to show which window is active and which are inactive. Ghost print in Workbench 1.3 signifies an inactive window. The reason for this difference is the mouse pointer.

The *multitasking* system of the Amiga causes this difference in active and inactive windows. Intuition recognizes the window in which you're working because clicking the mouse while in one window can have a completely different effect from clicking it in another. Active and inactive windows help the Amiga avoid conflicts between programs.

• Move the pointer anywhere inside the **Workbench** diskette window and click the left mouse button.

This activates the **Workbench** diskette window.

Notice the title line of the window and note the color of an active window in Workbench 2.0. You can now easily read the **Workbench** window title.

The top border is called the *drag bar*. It allows you to drag (move) the window to a new screen location.

- Move the pointer onto the drag bar of the **Workbench** window.

- Press and hold the left mouse button.

- Move the mouse around the screen.

- Release the left mouse button when the window is in the desired position.

A border appears as you move the mouse with the button depressed. This border helps you see whether the window you're moving would cover over any other windows. The entire window reappears when you release the left mouse button.

Window gadgets

Look at the upper right corner of the **Workbench** window. Notice the two boxes which appear side-by-side. We call these boxes *gadgets*. They control the status of the windows. Because these boxes operate differently in Workbench 2.0 and Workbench 1.3, we'll discuss each version separately.

Workbench 2.0 gadgets

Workbench 2.0 uses the left box of the upper right corner to toggle between a full screen window and the current window size. This is the *full size gadget*.

The right box is the *back/front gadget*. You'll use it to control the foreground and background status of the window. Clicking on this gadget toggles the window between the foreground and background.

- Move the pointer onto the System drawer icon.

- Double-click on the System drawer icon to open it.

This opens a new window called **System**.

- Move the pointer onto the drag bar (the top border) of the **System** window. Then press and hold the left mouse button.

- Drag (move) the **System** window so that it partially blocks the **Workbench** window. Then release the left mouse button.

Full Size gadget (2.0)

Notice that the window itself doesn't move. Only the border of the window shows the new location as you drag it around the screen. When you release the left mouse button, the window will move to the new location.

Look at the full size and back/front gadgets. The full size gadget is the left gadget in the upper right corner of the window and the back/front gadget is the right one.

- Click on the full size (left) gadget of the **System** window.

The full size gadget changes color for a moment before the size of the System window expands.

• Click on the full size (left) gadget of the System window once again.

The full size gadget changes color for a moment before the System window returns to its original size.

This gadget is very useful when working with multiple windows. It allows the active window to use the entire display and then easily return to its previous size and location. This gadget is not available in Workbench 1.3.

• Click on the Workbench diskette window to activate it.

Back/Front gadget (2.0)

• Click on the back/front (right) gadget of the Workbench diskette window.

The back/front gadget moved the System window behind the Workbench diskette window.

• Click the System window's front gadget to return it to the front.

The purpose of these gadgets is to allow you to page through overlapping windows as if they were sheets of paper. When a window disappears, it's normally moved to the back of the **Workbench** window.

Notice the difference between the **Workbench** diskette window and the **Workbench** window. Click on the **Workbench** window's back/front gadget to move the **Workbench** window to the background.

Other 2.0 gadgets

The System window's right border displays a long, thin box and another gadget in the lower right corner.

The long, thin box is called a *scroll bar*. Many windows may contain more files or information than what the screen displays. The scroll bar allows you to move or view inside these windows to look at the additional contents.

Another method of viewing additional files in the window is to use the *sizing gadget*. It is located at the bottom right corner of the window. It allows you to increase or reduce the size of the window.

• Move the pointer onto the System window's sizing gadget (the bottom right corner), press and hold the left mouse button.

• Drag the pointer up and to the left.

The window itself does not change size; only the size of the border changes. This is similar to when you dragged the window. The difference this time, however, is that moving the border up and to the left reduces the size of the window.

• Drag the sizing gadget toward the upper left corner. Release the left mouse button when the border is approximately two inches square.

When you release the left mouse button, the window will change to the same size as the border and at the same location.

One effect of reducing the size of the window is that the smaller size hides a part of the window. Now look at the bottom and right borders of the window. The scroll bars now appear white and blue. The white sections of the scroll bars represent the currently visible parts of the window. The scroll bars therefore also show how much of the total window is hidden from view.

There are two methods of using the scroll bars to move around a window:

• Move the pointer onto the blue section of a scroll bar and click on it.

• Move the pointer onto the white section of a scroll bar. Then press and hold the left mouse button. This allows you to drag the scroll bar in the blue area. Release the left mouse button when you're at the desired location.

As we mentioned, the scroll bars also show how much of the total window is hidden from view. This area is indicated by the blue shaded sections of the scroll bars.

The scroll bars work the same for both vertical and horizontal positions. Now enlarge the size of the window.

• Move the pointer onto the `System` window's sizing gadget. Press and hold the left mouse button.

• Drag the pointer down and to the right (the opposite direction from the close gadget).

• When you think the window is displaying all of its contents, release the left mouse button.

The way to confirm if the contents are completely displayed is to look at the right and bottom scroll bars. If neither bar show any blue shaded sections, then the window is back to full size.

You'll need to repeat these last three steps if there is still blue shaded sections visible in the scroll bars.

*Workbench
2.0 Title Bar*

The title bar of Workbench 2.0 diskettes also displays additional information about the open window. Diskette windows display the diskette name, the percentage of diskette space used, how much diskette space is free and how much diskette space is used. Drawer windows display the drawer name, the number of files, the number of directories and the number of blocks used in the drawer.

*Workbench
2.0 Drag
Select*

Workbench 2.0 also includes a feature called *Drag Select*. This allows you to quickly select several icons. This is very useful when you want to copy multiple files.

To start Drag Select, press and hold the left mouse button. As you move the mouse, a rectangle is drawn beginning from the original pointer location.

Continue moving the mouse until all of the icons you wish selected are either inside or touching the rectangle. Then release the mouse button. Then all icons are selected.

The right mouse button will cancel drag select mode.

*Workbench
1.3 gadgets*

Workbench 1.3 uses the boxes in the upper right hand corner of the window to control the foreground and background status of the window. Workbench 1.3 does not have a full size gadget. The left pair of boxes is the *back gadget*, and the right pair of boxes is the *front gadget*.

• Double click on the Workbench diskette icon. Move the pointer onto the System drawer icon.

• Double-click on the System drawer icon to open it.

A new window named **System** opens.

• Move the pointer onto the **System** window, and click on the window to make sure it is the active window.

• Move the pointer onto the drag bar (the top border) of the **System** window. Then press and hold the left mouse button.

• Drag (move) the **System** window so that it partially blocks the **Workbench** window. Then release the left mouse button.

*Workbench
1.3 front and
back gadgets*

Notice that the window itself doesn't move. Only the orange border of the window shows the new location as you drag it around the screen. When you release the left mouse button, the window will move to the new location.

Also notice the back and front gadgets. The back gadget has a black square in the foreground, and the front gadget has a white square in the foreground.

- Click on the front (right) gadget of the `System` window.

The only change is that the gadget changes color for a moment.

- Click on the back (left) gadget of the `System` window.

The back gadget changes color for a moment, and the `System` window seems to disappear.

- Click on the `Workbench` window to activate it.

- Move the pointer to the drag bar. Press and hold the left mouse button. Then drag the `Workbench` window down.

The back gadget moved the `System` window behind the `Workbench` window.

- Click the `System` window's front gadget to return it to the front.

These gadgets let you page through overlapping windows as if they were sheets of paper. The front gadget always brings windows to the front.

- Close the `System` window. This activates the `Workbench` window.

Other 1.3 gadgets

In the lower right border of the window is a long thin white box between two arrows. A gadget, resembling a pair of connected squares, is located in the lower right corner.

Many windows may contain more files or information than what is displayed on the screen. The arrows are *scroll arrows* and the thin box is a *scroll bar*. The scroll arrows and scroll bar allow you to move or view inside these windows to look at the additional contents.

Another method of viewing additional files in the window is to use the sizing gadget. It's located at the bottom right corner of the window. It allows you to increase or reduce the size of the window.

- Move the pointer onto the `Workbench` window's sizing gadget (the bottom right corner). Press and hold the left mouse button.

- Drag the pointer up and to the left.

The window itself does not change size; only the size of the orange border changes. This is similar to when you dragged the window. The difference this time, however, is that moving the border up and to the left reduces the size of the window.

• Drag the sizing gadget toward the upper left corner. When the border is approximately two inches square, release the left mouse button.

When you release the left mouse button, the window will change to the same size as the border and at the same location.

One effect of reducing the size of the window is that the smaller size hides a part of the window. Now look at the bottom and right borders of the window. The scroll bars now appear white and blue. The white sections of the scroll bars represent the currently visible parts of the window. The scroll bars therefore also show how much of the total window is hidden from view.

There are three ways to move around a window using the scroll arrows and scroll bars:

• Move the pointer onto the blue section of a scroll bar and click on it.

• Move the pointer onto the white section of a scroll bar. Then press and hold the left mouse button. This allows you to drag the scroll bar in the blue area. Release the left mouse button when you're at the desired location.

• Move the pointer and click on a scroll arrow closest to the blue section of a scroll bar.

As we mentioned, the scroll bars also show how much of the total window is hidden from view. This area is indicated by the blue shaded sections of the scroll bars.

The scroll bars work the same for both vertical and horizontal positions. Now enlarge the size of the window.

• Move the pointer onto the sizing gadget of the `Workbench` window. Then press and hold the left mouse button.

• Drag the pointer down and to the right (the opposite direction from the close gadget).

• When you think the window is displaying all of its contents, release the left mouse button.

The way to confirm if the full contents are displayed is to look at the right and bottom scroll bars. If neither bar show any blue shaded sections, then the window is back to full size.

Workbench 1.3 has two kinds of left window borders. Most left borders are narrow white lines. However, diskette windows display a *disk gauge* along their left borders.

The disk gauges indicate the amount of memory used on the diskette. Like a gas gauge on a car, E=empty and F=full. The orange bar rises as more data is stored on the diskette and falls when data is deleted from the diskette.

*Workbench
1.3 Extended
Selection*

Workbench 1.3 allows you to select multiple icons. This is very useful when you want to copy multiple files.

To start extended selection, press and hold either the left or right 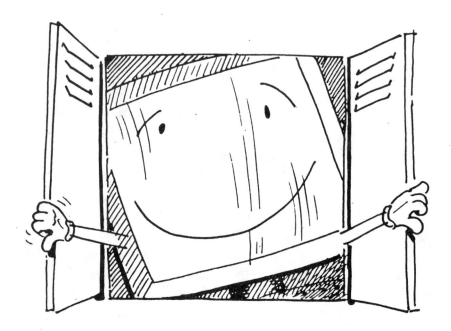 key. Icons can be selected as long as you hold the key down.

Press the left mouse button again to cancel extended selection.

2.4   The Clock

The Amiga has an excellent sense of timing. In fact, one of the popular
Amiga utilities is its working alarm clock. Look for an icon called
Clock inside the Utilities drawer.

- Double-click the Utilities drawer icon in the
  Workbench diskette window.

- Double-click the Clock icon.

You may hear the disk drive operate as the Amiga loads the program. In
a few moments an analog clock appears on the screen. Don't worry if
the time and date are incorrect. However, before setting the Clock,
experiment with the current **Clock** window:

- Move the pointer onto the sizing gadget of the **Clock** window.
  Press and hold the left mouse button.

- Drag the sizing gadget as far to the right as you can and release the
  left mouse button.

The clock expands in the direction you move the sizing gadget.

- Move the pointer onto the sizing gadget of the **Clock** window.
  Press and hold the left mouse button.

- Drag the sizing gadget back to its original position and release the
  left mouse button.

The Clock program has five pulldown menus:

Type

This offers you three different clock displays: Analog, Digital 1
and Digital 2. The Analog clock appears like a normal wall clock.
Its disadvantage is that it takes up too much space on the screen.

Therefore, you may prefer using the digital clocks. Digital 1 is a
standard digital display similar to a wristwatch. However, the display is
three times the height of the title bar and occupies almost as much
space as the analog clock window. Digital 2 has the smallest
display of the three clock types.

The Amiga defaults to the Analog clock, indicated by the left
checkmark of that menu item.

Workbench 2.0 offers only two options in this menu. `Digital` is the same as `Digital 1` mentioned above. `Analog` is also the same in Workbench 2.0 as it is in Workbench 1.3.

Mode

The **Mode** pulldown menu allows you to use either the 12 hour or 24 hour (world) time standards. The `Analog` 12 hour system displays AM or PM in the upper right hand corner of the **Clock** window. The two digital clocks display the AM or PM to the right of the time.

Seconds

This menu sets the seconds display on or off. The analog clock uses a second hand; the two digital displays use two-digit second displays. The Amiga clock defaults to `Seconds Off` which is indicated by the left checkmark of that menu item.

Date

Date sets the current date display on or off. The Amiga defaults to `Date Off` which is indicated by the left checkmark of that menu item.

Alarm

Alarm sets and activates or deactivates the Amiga alarm clock. `Set` opens the `Alarm Set` requester in which you set the alarm time. `Alarm On` and `Alarm Off` turn the alarm on and off. The Amiga defaults to `Alarm Off`. This is indicated by the left checkmark of that menu item.

Here are some experiments to help acquaint you with the clocks. First, select another clock type.

- Press and hold the right mouse button and move the pointer up to the **Type** menu title.

- Select the `Digital 2` item from the **Type** pulldown menu. (2.0 users should select the `Digital` item).

The `Analog` clock disappears and the smaller `Digital 2` clock appears.

- Press and hold the right mouse button and move the pointer up to the **Mode** menu title.

- Select the `24 Hour` item from the **Mode** pulldown menu.

The `Digital 2` clock changes to 24 hour mode (military time).

- Press and hold the right mouse button and move the pointer up to the **Date** menu title.

- Select the `Date On` item from the **Date** pulldown menu.

When `Date On` is selected, `Digital 2` alternates between date and time display. Each appears for about two seconds before changing to the other display.

- Select the Date Off item from the **Date** pulldown menu.

Digital 2 immediately stops displaying the date.

- Press and hold the right mouse button. Move the pointer up to the **Seconds** menu title.

- Select the Seconds On item from the **Seconds** pulldown menu.

Digital 2 now shows a two-digit second display.

- Press and hold the right mouse button and move the pointer up to the **Alarm** menu title.

- Select the Set item from the **Alarm** pulldown menu.

This displays a small requester called Alarm Set.

- Move the pointer onto the hour digits (the two left numbers).

- Click once so that the background behind the numbers changes.

- Move the pointer to the gadget containing the up and down arrows.

- Click twice on the up arrow of this gadget to move the time to 1400 hours.

- For setting minutes, click on the minute digits, and proceed as you did when you set hours.

- Click the Use gadget to set the alarm, or the Cancel gadget to cancel the setting.

You must turn the alarm on before it will go off at the prescribed time.

- Press and hold the right mouse button and move the pointer up to the **Alarm** menu title.

- Select the Alarm On item from the **Alarm** pulldown menu.

The alarm clock deactivates when you select Alarm Off from the **Alarm** pulldown menu.

- Select the Set item from the **Alarm** pulldown menu.

*Workbench
2.0*

The Alarm Set requester is slightly different in Workbench 2.0. Instead of arrows, you set the alarm using two vertical boxes. Notice the black selection button inside these two boxes. The left box displays the hours and the right box displays the minutes.

A smaller box will appear in the middle right of the Alarm Set requester if you're using a 12 hour display. It toggles between AM and PM.

- Move the pointer onto the black selection box in the hour display (left of the colon).

- Press and hold down the left mouse button. The black selection box changes to white.

- Move the pointer up or down to the hour the alarm should sound.

- Repeat these steps to set the minutes.

- If you're using a 12 hour clock, change the PM or AM setting if necessary. Move the mouse pointer to any location inside the AM/PM box and press the left mouse button.

- Click the Use gadget to set the alarm or the Cancel gadget to cancel the setting.

NOTE:

The Digital 2 clock has no alarm: Digital 2 ignores any alarm time input in the Set Alarm item of the **Alarm** pulldown menu. Analog and Digital 1 have functional alarms.

The clock itself still needs the proper time setting. The section on the use of Preferences explains setting the clock and more.

2.5   The System drawer

There are several *drawer* icons inside the Workbench window. These drawer icons open like diskette icons. Since the Amiga Workbench is an expanding system, some of the programs listed below may not appear in the drawers we discuss. If a program does not appear in the drawer mentioned, try looking in other drawers on the Workbench and Extras diskettes.

•   Double-click the System drawer icon to open it.

Wait pointer

As soon as you do this, the disk drive runs and the pointer changes into the wait pointer. This pointer is represented as clouds containing Zs in 1.3 or a clock face in 2.0. The System window appears on the screen.

This window may be inactive. You can tell if the window is inactive by the title. If it appears in ghost print, it's inactive.

•   Move the pointer into the System window.

A quick review of window components, going clockwise from the top left:

Close gadget: click on this gadget to close the window.

Drag bar: displays the title and lets you drag (move) the window around the screen.

Full size gadget: for sizing a window to the full screen (only the back gadget appears in 1.3).

Back/Front gadget: for bringing a window in back of or in front of another window (only the front gadget appears in 1.3).

Right scroll bar: for moving around vertically inside a window. Workbench 1.3 also has scroll arrows.

Sizing gadget: for reducing and enlarging the size of a window.

Bottom scroll bar: for moving around horizontally inside a window. Workbench 1.3 also has scroll arrows.

Title bar displays the amount of free and used disk space. Workbench 1.3 has a Disk gauge which tells the amount of memory used on a diskette (appears on disk windows only).

The System drawer contains a number of useful programs. One of the most important is the Diskcopy program which lets you copy diskettes.

- If you haven't opened the System drawer yet, double click on its icon.

A window opens. As we mentioned, the **System** window contains a number of programs. For now, two programs are of the most interest:

The first is named Diskcopy.

The second is named Format.

Formatting disks

Initialize and *format* mean the same thing when talking about floppy diskettes. Both terms describe how a computer prepares a diskette to accept data. Say you have a diskette with data which you no longer need or you buy a diskette from the store. The computer prepares the diskette so that you can put new information on it by formatting or initializing the diskette.

Every Amiga disk drive has a magnetic head that deletes any information on a diskette. This magnetic head also creates the new *tracks* and *sectors* required for saving information. However, once the computer formats a diskette, any data previously on a diskette is lost forever. Therefore, if you format previously used diskettes, be absolutely sure that you'll never need the information on them again. This warning doesn't apply new diskettes, since they obviously have no information on them anyway.

Perhaps you want to know why new diskettes need formatting. Each diskette manufacturer wants to sell to as many computer users as possible. Therefore, they sell "blank" diskettes which every computer, regardless of manufacturer, can use. The computer adapts blank diskettes by formatting (initializing).

WARNING:

Formatting a previously formatted diskette destroys all data previously stored on that diskette.

We'll assume that you only have one disk drive. The procedures are basically the same if you have two drives. The main difference is that the Amiga won't constantly prompt you to change diskettes. When formatting with two drives, place the Workbench diskette in the internal disk drive (drive 0) and the new diskette into the external drive (drive 1). The Amiga 2000 and 3000 may contain two internal disk drives, we'll always refer to the second disk drive as the external disk drive.

WARNING: **NEVER remove a diskette from the drive while the disk drive LED is on. The Amiga may destroy all the data on that disk.** If you do, go to Appendix A for instructions on using the `Diskdoctor` program. This program might rescue some of the data.

- Double-click the `Format` icon.

Requesters

A *requester* appears. A requester, as the name suggests, tells you of a problem, error or unfinished task. It also prompts or requests specific information or data. For example, requesters tell you to change diskettes.

It's important to follow the information of the requester. Otherwise you may risk a *system crash*. This means that the computer restarts itself and loses all the input since you last saved the data and information.

This requester tells you to select the icon of the diskette you want formatted. If you're using Workbench 2.0, you must select `Format` from the `Icon` menu. Workbench 1.3 users are requested to select `Initialize` from the **Disk** menu.

- Click on the `OK` gadget to continue.

- Remove the Workbench diskette from the disk drive and replace it with a blank diskette. A new diskette icon appears as `DF0:` in Workbench 2.0 and this icon is named `DF0:BAD` for Workbench 1.3 users.

- Click on the diskette icon you want initialized (usually `DF0:` or `DF0:BAD` for 1.3 users).

The icon changes color, indicating an active icon. Go to the **Icon** menu and select the Format Disk... item (1.3 users select the **Disk** menu and the `Initialize` item). A requester appears asking you to replace the Workbench diskette. Remove the blank diskette and insert the Workbench diskette. The formatting program will be loaded and then a requester appears asking you to insert the diskette to be initialized. DO NOT REMOVE THE WORKBENCH DISKETTE WHEN THE DRIVE LIGHT IS STILL ON. Wait for the drive light to go off.

Insert disk requester

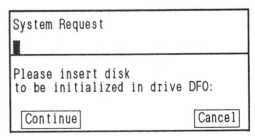

```
System Request
▮
─────────────────────────────────
Please insert disk
to be initialized in drive DF0:

 ┌──────────┐            ┌──────┐
 │ Continue │            │Cancel│
 └──────────┘            └──────┘
```

Once you have the diskette in the drive select the `Continue` gadget. After a short period of time another requester appears verifying the initialization of the diskette. If you're positive you have the correct diskette in the drive, click on the `Continue` gadget. The Amiga asks this to ensure that you don't accidentally delete important information.

Even if you have the correct diskette, you may want to reconsider formatting this diskette. Remember, all data on the diskette is lost when formatting. If you're absolutely sure that you want this disk formatted, then:

- Click on the `Continue` gadget in the requester.

Ok to
Initialize
requester

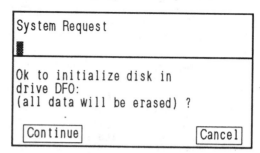

As soon as you give the Amiga the OK to initialize, the requester changes to a window displaying the status of the initializing process.

You may be wondering why two diskette icons appear on the screen when you only have one disk drive. The Amiga keeps the icons of the Workbench diskette and the new `DF0:` diskette in memory. There may be a third diskette icon, called `RAM Disk`, on the screen (more on this later).

One hint for two disk drive Amiga owners: When your Amiga requests a certain diskette to be inserted in "any" drive, it usually means the internal disk drive. Therefore, if you inserted the disk into "any drive" and nothing happened, remove the requested diskette and insert it in the internal drive.

You'll hear the disk drive make some noise. Soon the Amiga displays the message `DF0:BUSY` below the selected diskette icon. This means that the built-in drive (known internally as `DF0:`) is performing a disk operation (=BUSY).

The disk drive stops after a short time. Notice instead of `DF0:BUSY`, the diskette icon has the name `Empty` underneath it. You've just formatted your first Amiga diskette.

- Double-click the `Empty` diskette icon.

A window named **Empty** opens. The **Empty** window contains only one icon; the `Trashcan` (more on this later). Otherwise, the **Empty** window looks and acts exactly like any other diskette window.

• Close the **Empty** window and remove the `Empty` diskette from the drive.

Copying diskettes

The following instructions explain how to copy the Workbench diskette using the `Diskcopy` program. Copying diskettes safeguards you from unpleasant surprises. It doesn't take much to accidentally erase an important file, or spill coffee on the Workbench diskette. Always make *backup copies* of diskettes. Backup copies are copies of an original diskette. Use backups for your work, and keep the original diskettes in a safe, non-magnetic place.

Make sure to enable the *write protect* on your Workbench diskette. The write protect is the small sliding piece of plastic in one corner of a floppy diskette. If you can see through the write protect hole, you can't write to the diskette.

Write Enable   Write Protect

Write protect

• Move the write protect slider on the Workbench diskette so you can see through the hole (write protect it).

• Insert your Workbench diskette in the internal disk drive.

• Click on the `Workbench` diskette icon.

• Press and hold the ⏷ key (Shift key). Double-click the `Diskcopy` icon in the **System** window and release the ⏷ key.

Extended Selection

This process of holding the ⏷ key (Shift key) down while selecting icons is *extended selection*. Extended selection lets you select two or more icons at a time.

A requester similar to the following appears:

Disk Copy
Source
requester

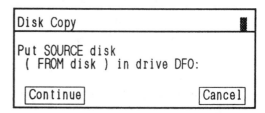

- Click on the Continue gadget. The Amiga reads in part of the disk to be copied.

Another requester appears asking you to insert the destination diskette (the blank diskette to which you're copying):

- Insert a blank diskette and click on the Continue gadget. The Amiga writes to the disk to be copied.

Disk Copy
Destination
requester

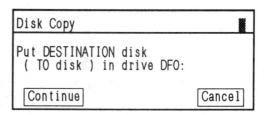

- Click on the Continue gadget.

The Amiga tells you which diskette it needs through requesters.

Two-drive
copying

A two disk drive Amiga system requires no diskette changes when copying. The procedure has only a few changes than copying diskettes with one drive. If you're using two disk drives, follow this procedure:

- Move the write protect slider on the Workbench diskette so you can see through the hole (enable write protection).

- Insert the original Workbench diskette into the internal disk drive, and the blank diskette into the external disk drive.

- Click on the Workbench diskette icon.

- Press and hold one of the two ⇧ keys.

- Click on the diskette icon representing the external disk drive. The name is probably DF1: or DF1:BAD if this diskette is blank.

- Double-click the Diskcopy icon in the **System** window and release the ⇧ key.

- Follow the Amiga's instructions through the requesters and click on the proper gadgets to continue.

- Use the above instructions to make backup copies of the Extras diskette which came with your Amiga.

- Close the System drawer when you finish making backup copies.

Now that you have a backup of the Workbench diskette, we'll test it by resetting the computer:

- Insert your backup copy of the Workbench diskette into the Amiga's internal disk drive.

- Simultaneously press the [Ctrl] key (on the far left of the keyboard), the <Commodore logo> key (or the left <Amiga> key) and the right <Amiga> key.

The Amiga acts as if you switched it on. The screen turns gray, it reads your Workbench diskette and displays the Workbench screen.

Storing original diskettes

If your backup diskettes work, take your original diskettes and put them in a safe place. "A safe place" means a location shielded from extreme heat and cold, far away from magnetic objects, food and drink, animals and children. Use your original diskettes only if you need to make copies. However, since you can always make backups of backups, you may never have to get your originals out again.

CLI

The **System** window displays a few other programs. For example, a box icon containing >1 and the name CLI. This is the Command Line Interface. If you don't see this icon, don't worry about it; you won't need it for a while. If there is such an icon, leave it alone for now (see Chapter 4 for information on the CLI).

FixFonts

New fonts for the Amiga appear frequently from Commodore. The FixFonts program is used when fonts are added or deleted on the Workbench diskette. FixFonts checks and corrects the files that tell the Amiga which fonts it has available for use. Try running this program if you have any problems using or loading fonts. It will update your Workbench so the Amiga can access all available fonts.

NoFastMem

This program rearranges the memory of the Amiga to allow older programs written for the Amiga 1000 to work on the new Amigas. If programs (especially games) do not seem to work correctly, try running NoFastMem before loading these programs.

InitPrinter

This program updates the printer to the one you have selected in Preferences. See the section on Preferences for more info.

SetMap

The SetMap program allows the Amiga to access special and foreign characters from the keyboard, as well as assign specific character sets to the keyboard. This allows the loading of different international keyboard definitions into the Amiga.

Remember that the Amiga Workbench is an ever expanding and improving system. Programs are changed and added to the Workbench to upgrade and improve the Amiga operating system. Therefore the programs listed in this book may not appear in the drawers or diskettes listed. If a program does not appear in the drawer mentioned, try looking in other drawers on the Workbench and Extras diskettes for the program.

2.6   The Utilities drawer

The Utilities drawer contains the Amiga utility programs. Several new utilities were added to the Workbench 2.0 system. We'll first discuss the programs which are available only on the Workbench 1.3 system before discussing the programs available on both 1.3 and 2.0. In the last part of this section, we'll discuss the new utility programs available only for Workbench 2.0 users.

•   Double-click on the Utilities drawer icon to open the drawer.

Notepad
V1.3   only

The Notepad gives you some idea of the capabilities of even the simplest Amiga *word processor*. A word processor lets you write text, similar to working with a typewriter. That's where the similarity ends. Word processing also allows you to move, delete, rewrite and edit text on the screen.

Calculator
V1.3 & V2.0

The Calculator utility opens like any other program. Since it is a window, you can place it in front of or behind other windows.

The Amiga calculator works exactly like a pocket calculator except it has some special features:

1.   You can access calculator functions from both the mouse and the Amiga keyboard. For special functions such as CE, press the necessary letter keys (press the Ⓒ key and then the Ⓔ key). The (Enter) key on the keypad is the same as the equal sign on the calculator.

2.   This Calculator has a delete function. Click on the ⬅ key (on the bottom row of the **Calculator** window) to delete numeric input from right to left. Pressing the (Backspace) key, ⬅ key, or the (Del) key on the keyboard also deletes numbers from the calculator.

3.   The CE function lets you clear only the last entry. For example, if you make a mistake entering a number, click CE. This deletes the current input while retaining the previous computation in memory. Click CA (Clear All) when you want to start a new calculation.

•   Double-click the Notepad icon.

Clock
V1.3 & V2.0

The Clock displays the current time and date on your Amiga. For more information on the Clock, see Chapter 2.4.

Cmd
V1.3 & V2.0

The Cmd program will redirect output that normally goes to the serial port or parallel port to a file. This allows you to capture printer output to a file. The default parameters are defined in the tool type of the **Info** window.

- Double click the Cmd icon.

Although it appears nothing has happened, if you try to print anything it will now be sent to the RAM: disk with the name CMD_File.

- Double click the Cmd icon again.

A window will be displayed informing you that the redirection has been removed.

Graphic-Dump
V1.3 & V.2.0

The GraphicDump program produces *hardcopies* (printouts) of the screen contents. You can only use this program if your printer prints graphics. If you have a printer connected and operating:

- Double-click the GraphicDump icon.

The printer reproduces the screen picture on paper. GraphicDump waits 10 seconds after your double-click before it starts printing, so you have some time to move screens or windows where you want them.

More
V1.3 & V2.0

More is used to display documents called ASCII text files (American Standard Code for Information Interchange). When text completely fills the screen, More pauses until you press a key. The document is not displayed further until you press a key.

- Double click the More icon and enter the following:

      SYS:S/startup-sequence

- Press the ⏎ key.

This displays a sequence of commands. This is the start up sequence that the Amiga executes when it is switched on. Don't worry if these commands look confusing; it's only important that your Amiga understands them. Press any key to return to the Workbench.

printfiles
V1.3 & V2.0

The Printfiles program allows you to print multiple files from the Workbench. Select the files while holding down one of the two ⬆ keys and then start the Printfiles program. Your files will be printed to the printer selected in Preferences. See the section on Preferences for more information on selecting a printer.

Say
V1.3 & V2.0

The Say program demonstrates the Amiga's speech synthesis.

- Double-click on the Say icon.

The **Phoneme** window opens and displays the various options available.

A second window (the **Input** window) appears below this one. The Amiga converts everything you type in this window into speech.

• Click inside the **Input** window.

• Enter the following from the keyboard:

    Hello, user. I'm your Amiga.

• Press the ⏎ key.

Commodore Amiga programmers wrote the speech synthesizer to imitate the English language as closely as possible, but some words just don't come out right. Say's pronunciation improves when you spell the word phonetically instead of literally. Say not only says what you type in; it also lets you change the Amiga's voice.

• Enter -s400 and press the ⏎ key.

• Enter Peter Piper picked a peck of pickled peppers.

• Press the ⏎ key.

You must enter speed or pitch changes before entering the specific text. Precede all speech changes with a dash (-) and the corresponding letter as listed in the **Phoneme** window. Pitch and speed changes also require a number. Acceptable speeds range from 40 to 400 and pitches range from 65 to 320. Experiment with the different parameters.

• Press the ⏎ key without entering anything to end the program.

Exchange
V2.0 only

The Commodities Exchange program allows programmers to customize the input settings of the Workbench. When Commodities Exchange programs are started the Exchange program keeps track of them and can be used to enable or disable them. Those included with Workbench 2.0 are:

Autopoint which will automatically activate a window when the mouse pointer is moved onto the window. No more tedious clicking. This type of mouse pointer is know as a "Sun Pointer", after the company that uses this type of pointer in its graphic work stations.

• Double click on the Autopoint icon.

Move the mouse pointer around the display, notice that the window under the mouse is automatically activated when the pointer moves across it.

Blanker is a screen blanker program. This allows you to turn off (or clear) the screen after a specified amount of time when you have not used the keyboard. The default time is 60 seconds.

The Ihelp program enables the Intuition keyboard help functions.

* Double click on the Ihelp icon.

Nothing seems to happen. Press all of the function keys, one at a time, and note what happens to the active window. Ihelp is used to provide keyboard control of Intuition.

Nocapslock disables the [Caps Lock] key which is great for the touch typist.

Fkey allows you to define the functions keys for use in programs or in the Amiga Shell. You can enter twenty function key definitions; the ten function keys alone or the function keys using the [⬆] keys.

* Double click on the Ihelp icon.

The function key definition window is displayed. The function key definition window can be called by the hotkey sequence [Alt] + [F1] keys.

* Double click on the Exchange program.

This displays the active Commodities Exchange programs. The Exchange program displays information on the available commodities. It also allows you to Enable, Disable and Kill commodities. You can Hide or Quit the Exchange program. When you select commodities, you can show or hide their respective windows. The function key definition window can be called by the hotkey sequence [Alt] + [F1] keys.

Memacs
V2.0 only

The Memacs program is a full feature text editing program, similar to a word processor but without all the bells and whistles. The EMACS editor is popular on mainframe computers and this is a smaller or MicroEmacs version of this popular editor.

2.7   An Intuition glossary

This book uses many words that may be new to you. The summary in this section defines terms used when discussing Intuition.

Active

An active window or pulldown menu item will appear in clear and legible type. Inactive window titles and pulldown menu items display ghost print (gray and hard-to-read). Active pulldown menu items have dark backgrounds as you pass the mouse pointer over them. Active icons also turn dark when selected. Items, windows and icons all activate when clicked one or more times with the mouse. Active menu items have checkmarks next to them.

Clicking

This is how you select and activate programs and icons. The term clicking is the act of pressing the left mouse button. A single click turns an icon black, while a double-click activates the programs represented by the icon.

Double-clicking

Double-clicking loads programs and opens windows. You need to move the pointer onto the desired icon and press the left mouse key twice in rapid succession.

Dragging

As you use your Amiga, you'll occasionally need to move windows and icons. For example, move the pointer onto the icon, or onto the window's drag bar, and press and hold the left mouse button. As you move the mouse (still pressing the left mouse button), the selected object moves with it. When the object reaches the desired position, release the left mouse button.

Drag Select

Workbench 2.0 also includes a feature called Drag Select. This allows you to easily select several icons. To start Drag Select, simply press and hold the left mouse button and then move the mouse. A rectangle appears starting from the original location of the pointer. All icons inside or touching the rectangle are selected when you release the mouse button. This is very useful when you want to copy multiple files. Press the right mouse button to cancel the drag select mode.

Drawers

Drawers contain related programs and files. For example, the Demos drawer contains all the Workbench demonstration programs.

Enlarging

In principle, this function works exactly like dragging. Place the pointer on the sizing gadget in the lower right corner of the window. Press and hold the left mouse button and drag the sizing gadget away from the upper left corner of the window. The window size changes in the direction of the pointer movement.

Extended
Selection

This process of holding down one of the 🔲 keys while selecting icons is *extended selection*. Extended selection lets you select two or more icons at a time.

Gadgets

Gadgets are objects built into windows to help you move, adjust and manage windows.

Sizing gadgets enlarge or reduce window sizes. Scroll bars and scroll arrows move the contents of the window around, so you can see programs and drawers not visible in the normal window.

The back/front gadget is in the upper right of the window drag bar. If you click the back/front gadget, you can move a window to the background. When you click the back/front gadget a second time, the window moves to the foreground.

The gadget to the right of the back/front gadget, is the full size gadget and is only available on Workbench 2.0. Workbench 1.3 uses the two gadgets as a back gadget and a front gadget.

You can move windows with the drag bar (the top border of a window). Move the pointer onto the drag bar. Then press and hold the left mouse key, which allows window movement.

Close gadgets (the small box with a dot in its center, in the upper left corner of the window) close windows.

Icon

Icons are pictures on the Amiga screen. They can be tools (programs), projects (files) or drawers. Other objects such as the `Trashcan` or pictures of diskettes are also icons.

Info bar

The info bar is a horizontal bar across the top of the screen. It displays the amount of free memory or the current version of the Workbench diskette. The Amiga can operate several screen planes at once. In addition, when pressing the right mouse button, the info bar displays menu titles. Certain selections and programs can affect and therefore change the info bar (the `Version` is an example).

Information
window

Every icon has an information window. This window list filenames, file size, comments, etc. Diskette information windows list the amount of free memory on the diskette.

Memory meter

This line contains the screen name and the amount of free memory in the Amiga. It appears across the top of the screen when in the Workbench.

Menu item

Menu items are individual commands located below menu titles.

Menu titles

Pressing the right mouse button activates menu titles at the top of the screen. Each menu title contains a list of menu items for user selection.

Open

Tools (programs) and projects (files and documents) open or execute. When you double-click a project, the tool used to create the project also opens.

Options

These are additional menu options coming from menu items.

Program

Everything the Amiga does has its basis in a program. However, with Intuition running, programs generally perform a service and allow user access from Intuition (see also *Tools*).

Project

Projects are data files generated from inside a program.

Pulldown menu

You select pulldown menus by pressing the right mouse button. If you press and hold this button, a set of menu titles appear at the top of the screen. A pulldown menu listing a number of items appears when you move the pointer onto one of the menu titles. Move the pointer onto the desired menu item. The selected menu item executes when you release the right mouse button.

Reducing

In principle, this function works exactly like enlarging. Move the pointer on the sizing gadget in the lower right corner of the window. Then press and hold the left mouse button and drag the sizing gadget toward the upper left corner of the window. The window size changes in the direction of the pointer movement.

Requester

Requesters are windows of different sizes, different texts and gadgets. These requesters all have one thing in common: They ensure that the Amiga obtains the information it needs for performing certain tasks. For example, if you want a diskette copied onto another one, the Amiga must know the difference between the original diskette and the destination diskette. It requests this information using a requester. These requesters include gadgets for user response.

Tools

Tools help you and the Amiga perform certain tasks. Basically, you could call the Workbench and Intuition tools. Programmers and people with full knowledge of computers define a tool as a program that helps the user program. For example, since Diskcopy copies diskettes, it's considered a tool. There are tools for users at all levels, from the new user to the expert programmer.

User interface

The entire Amiga screen area is a user interface. The user interface of a computer varies in size and user-friendliness, depending on the task it performs. You presently know only one user interface on the Amiga (the Workbench). The Amiga can manage several user interfaces at the same time.

Window

Windows can contain data or programs which you can start or view. In addition, windows have gadgets which perform different functions (see gadgets).

2.8   The Trashcan

The Amiga's Trashcan acts as a file disposal. When you no longer need a drawer, tool, project or program, drag it to the Trashcan. For demonstration purposes, make a copy of the Clock program using the Copy function of the Icon menu. Workbench 1.3 user should use the Duplicate function of the Workbench menu.

- Double-click the Utilities drawer.

- Select the Clock icon.

- Select the Copy function of the **Icon** menu. Workbench 1.3 users should use the Duplicate function of the **Workbench** menu.

A new file named Copy of Clock appears in the Utilities window.

- Make sure the Trashcan icon is visible in the Workbench diskette window. Move around inside the window with the scroll arrows and scroll bars until you find the Trashcan icon.

- Move the pointer onto the Copy of Clock icon, press and hold the left mouse button.

- Drag the Copy of Clock icon until it covers the Trashcan icon in the Workbench diskette window.

- Release the left mouse button.

The Amiga's disk drive runs. The file still exists, though. If you look at the Workbench diskette's info window, the amount of available memory has decreased. The Copy of Clock file is in the Trashcan for now.

- Double-click the Trashcan icon.

A window named Trashcan opens. The Copy of Clock icon appears in this window. This lets you remove any file in the Trashcan before you dispose of it by mistake.

- Move the pointer onto the Copy of Clock icon, press and hold the left mouse button.

- Drag the Copy of Clock icon back to the Utilities window and release the left mouse button.

Now that you know how to remove files from the Trashcan, dispose of the Copy of Clock permanently.

*   Move the pointer onto the Copy of Clock icon, press and hold the left mouse button.

*   Drag the Copy of Clock icon until it covers the Trashcan icon in the Workbench window.

*   Release the left mouse button.

The disk drive runs again.

*   Activate the Trashcan icon.

*   Select the Empty Trash item from the **Icon** pulldown menu (**Disk** in Workbench 1.3)

The disk drive runs again. The memory meter increases and the Copy of Clock disappears. Activating the Trashcan icon before you can Empty Trash gives you one last chance to think before you dispose of the Trashcan's contents. You can put almost anything into the Trashcan, but not diskette icons.

NOTE: **Be extremely careful when using the Trashcan. Once you select Empty Trash, the file you trash is gone forever.**

2.9   Preferences 2.0

Preferences 2.0 is one of the Workbench's most powerful features. You can install and adjust nearly any Amiga setting to your individual preference. Preferences is a program in Workbench 1.3 but Workbench 2.0 contains a drawer named Prefs that is filled with individual programs. The Prefs drawer contain programs that make up Preferences. This is a flexible and important upgrade from Workbench 1.3.

This is one of the major improvements between Workbench 1.3 and Workbench 2.0. Therefore we'll explain the Workbench 2.0 programs which make up Preferences in this section.

We'll discuss the Workbench 1.3 Preferences program in Section 2.10.

Workbench 2.0 Preferences

- Double-click the Workbench diskette window to open it.

- Double-click the Prefs drawer icon in the Workbench diskette window.

The window which opens will contain the following programs: Font, Icontrol, Input, Overscan, Palette, Pointer, Printer, Printergfx, Serial, Wbpattern and Wbscreen. The list may also include other programs. These individual programs make up the Workbench 2.0 Preferences.

Preference Program Menus

Most of the Preference programs share a common menu system. This menu allows you to edit, cancel and save all of the choices you have made. This is a great enhancement over the earlier versions of the Workbench. Since these menus are common to most preferences programs, we'll only discuss them one time.

- Double click on the Font program to start it.

- Once the Font program is loaded (the Font Preferences window is displayed), press the right mouse button to display the menu.

The following menus are displayed:

```
Project          Edit                Options
Open...           Reset to Default    Save Icons?
Save As...        Last Saved
Quit              Restore
```

The Project menu allows you to load (Open) and save (Save as) your preference choices. The default filename is the name of the program followed by a .pre extension. The default filename has a prefs extension if the saved preferences are loaded when you first switch on your Amiga. These files are located in the prefs/env-archive subdirectory.

Quit is identical to clicking on the close gadget and will end the program.

The Edit menu provides you with three options. You can restore the system to its default values (Reset to defaults), to the last saved changes (Last Saved) or restore the system to the values before you called the program (Restore).

The Options menu allows you to save the changes to a file which has a corresponding icon (Save Icons). As you double-click this icon, the program will start and loads the saved values. You cannot save an icon if the Save Icons item is ghosted because the saved preferences for these programs are loaded when you first switch on your Amiga.

Save
Use
Cancel

Most of the preferences program contain the gadgets Save, Use and Cancel. Since these gadgets are common to most preferences program we'll only discuss them one time.

The Save gadget stores your changes to diskette. You should only do this on a copy of the Workbench diskette (not the original). The default filename is the name of the program followed by a .pre extension. If the saved preferences are loaded when the Amiga is first turned on the default filename has a prefs extension. These files are located in the prefs/env-archive subdirectory.

The Use gadget tells the Amiga to use these changes but *does not* save the changes to disk.

The Cancel gadget exits the current running program without saving or using any of the changes. The Workbench reappears with the original settings.

Font

This program allows you to change the fonts used by the Workbench. You may choose which font to use for icon text, screen text and the system default text.

• Double-click the fonts icon in the Prefs window.

A window will appear listing the available fonts on your Workbench diskette. If only a few fonts appear on this list, refer to CLI Tricks and Tips in Chapter 4. We'll discuss how to copy all the fonts on the Extras diskette to your Workbench diskette.

You can see examples of the different fonts by selecting the font. Try experimenting with different fonts and colors. Select the Use gadget to use your new selections. Be careful, however, because the Amiga follows your instructions and larger fonts and color combinations may be unreadable.

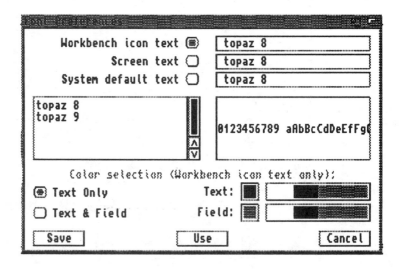

Font
Preferences
Window

Continue until you are satisfied with the screen display. Then select the Save gadget to store your font selections.

The Save gadget stores your changes to diskette. You should only do this on a copy of the Workbench diskette (not the original). The default filename is Font.pre. You can always save these to diskette later on in this session if you want to keep these changes.

The Use gadget tells the Amiga to use these changes but *does not* save the changes to disk.

The Cancel gadget exits the Font program without saving or using any of the changes. The Workbench reappears with the original settings.

Icontrol

This program set several Intuition specific control items. These include Verify Timeout, Command keys, Mouse screen drag, Coercion and Miscellaneous Flags.

```
 Verify Timeout        Command Keys              Mouse
  .5 Second  ○       A  N  : WB screen to front   Screen Drag
  1.0 Second ◉       A  M  : Front screen to back  Shft □
  1.5 Seconds ○      A  V  : Requester OK          Ctrl □
  2.0 Seconds ○      A  B  : Requester CANCEL      Alt  □
  5.0 Seconds ○                                     A   ☑
           Coercion            Miscellaneous Flags
       Avoid flicker: ☑      Screen menu snap: ☑
       Preserve colors: ☑    Text gadget filter: ☑
  [ Save ]              [ Use ]                 [ Cancel ]
```

*IControl
Preferences
Window*

Command keys allows you to combine certain keys with the Amiga key to perform common Amiga actions. You can select the key to move the Workbench screen to the front and to move the front screen to the back, useful when running multiple programs on your multitasking Amiga. It's possible to select the OK and Cancel gadgets of many requesters directly from the keyboard. Icontrol allows you to select the keys to select these gadgets in a requester.

There are situations where a program waits for a response from Intuition at the same time Intuition is waiting for a response from the same program. Verify timeout gadget allows you to wait for a response from another program. If no response is received in a specified time period, Intuition proceeds and avoids a system crash.

The time period you can specify are .5, 1, 1.5, 2 or 5 seconds. We recommend using either 2 or 5 seconds. This longer period of time will give your Amiga an opportunity to work out the problem itself.

Mouse screen drag allows you to select the Shift (⬆), Ctrl (Ctrl), Alt (Alt) or A (<Amiga>) keys to use with the mouse to drag the screen. This gadget allows you to use keys in addition to or in place of the left <Amiga> key. For example, by selecting Alt, you must press the Alt key and use the mouse to drag the screen.

Miscellaneous Flags option is for users who work with screens which exceed the width of the display area of the monitor. If the left most part of the Amiga screen is not visible on your monitor screen, select Screen menu snap.

The Save gadget stores your changes to diskette. You should only do this on a copy of the Workbench diskette (not the original). The default filename is IControl.pre. You can always save these changes to diskette later in this session.

The Use gadget tells the Amiga to use these changes but *does not* save the changes to disk.

The Cancel gadget exits the Icontrol program without saving or using any of the changes. The Workbench reappears with the original settings.

Input

Input program controls the user input speed of the keyboard and the mouse.

The Mouse Speed gadget is used to control the speed of mouse movement.

Input Preferences Window

Input Preferences

```
                        Mouse
     Mouse Speed:        1      [████████        ]
     Acceleration:              [   ]
     Double-Click:    1.02 sec  [      ■         ]
        [ Show ] [   ]                    [ Test ]

                      Keyboard
   Key Repeat Delay:   0.60 sec  [         ■      ]
   Key Repeat Rate:   0.050 sec  [        ■       ]
   Key Repeat Test:            [                  ]
   [   Save   ]        [    Use    ]      [ Cancel ]
```

- Move the pointer onto the Mouse Speed slider (the small box in the gadget).

- Press and hold the left mouse button.

- Drag the slider all the way to the right. The display will read 4. The 4 setting is the slowest speed for the pointer.

- Move the pointer onto the Mouse Speed slider.

- Press and hold the left mouse button.

- Drag the slider all the way to the left. The display will read 1. The mouse will now move very fast.

The Acceleration gadget is used to control the acceleration of the pointer in relation to mouse movement.

- Select the Acceleration gadget, a check mark (√) appears in the gadget when acceleration is on.

Now when you move the mouse, the pointer will accelerate in relation to the distance you move the mouse.

The Double-Click sliding gadget is used to control the time required to double-clicking on an icon to select it. The Show gadget shows the amount of time selected.

- Move the pointer onto the `Double-Click` slider (the small box in the gadget).

- Press and hold the left mouse button.

- Drag the slider all the way to the left. The display will read 0.20 seconds.

- Select the Show gadget. The box next to the gadget will change colors for the amount of time specified in the `Double-Click` gadget.

- Try double clicking on the Test gadget. It's almost impossible at 0.20 seconds.

- Move the pointer onto the `Double-Click` slider (the small box in the gadget).

- Press and hold the left mouse button.

- Drag the slider until the display reads 1.02 seconds to return to the default rate.

The `Key Repeat Delay` gadget adjusts the time delay between a key press and the key repeat. The Amiga waits for the amount of time you set here between your pressing a key and the first key repetition.

- Move the pointer onto the `Key Repeat Delay` dark box of the slider.

- Press and hold the left mouse button.

- Drag the slider all the way to the left. The display will read 0.20 seconds.

- Press and hold down the Ⓐ key on the keyboard. This displays an "a" in the `Key Repeat Test` gadget. The letter repeats almost immediately.

- Move the pointer onto the `Key Repeat Delay` dark box of the slider.

- Press and hold the left mouse button.

- Drag the slider all the way to the right. The display will read 1.5 seconds.

- Press and hold down the Ⓐ key on the keyboard. An "a" is displayed in the Key Repeat Test gadget. The Amiga waits 1.5 seconds before repeating the key.

The Key Repeat Speed gadget adjusts the speed at which keys repeat when held down. For example, if you press and hold a key in the CLI, the Amiga waits a moment then prints the letter until you release the key.

- Move the pointer onto the Key Repeat Speed slider.

- Press and hold the left mouse button.

- Drag the slider all the way to the right. The display will read 0.250 seconds.

- Press and hold down the Ⓐ key on the keyboard. An "a" is displayed in the Key Repeat Test gadget. The letter repeats very slowly.

- Move the pointer onto the Key Repeat Speed slider.

- Press and hold the left mouse button.

- Drag the slider all the way to the left. The display will read 0.002 seconds.

- Press and hold down the Ⓐ key on the keyboard. An "a" is displayed in the Key Repeat Test gadget. The letter repeats very quickly.

The Save gadget stores your changes to diskette. You should only save this on a copy of the Workbench diskette (not the original). The default filename is input.prefs. This file is located in the prefs/env-archive subdirectory. You can always save these to diskette later on in this session if you want to keep them.

The Use gadget tells the Amiga to use these changes but *does not* save the changes to disk.

The Cancel gadget exits the Input program without saving or using any of the changes. The Workbench reappears with the original settings.

Overscan

Most computers limit their display to a central area of your monitor screen. This leaves a colored border around the edges. Normal video signals will fill the entire screen (plus a bit more to accommodate the variety and sizes of television picture tubes). Overscan is when you use the entire Amiga screen.

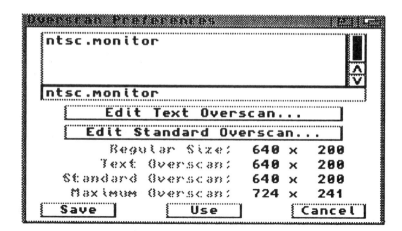

*Overscan
Preferences
Window*

Unless you're using your Amiga for desktop video, you probably won't need to use the overscan mode. The overscan mode is used to allow the excellent text and graphics created on your Amiga to be transferred to video tape. The overscan modes allow you to use the entire display screen, not just the center portion.

The Overscan program will display the monitor types and the overscan modes available. Most Amiga users will only have the `default monitor` available. If you have installed a special video card in your Amiga then you will probably have other monitor types available. The modes available in the `default monitor` are `Lores`, `Hires`, `320 x 200`, `Lores-Interlaced`, `Hires-Interlaced` and `320 x 400 Interlaced`.

`Edit Text Overscan` and `Edit Standard Overscan` will allow you to edit the size of the overscan display. Selecting either of these shows the overscan display. You can size the overscan area by using the selection rectangle. Press the (Esc) key to exit either of these modes.

Show Overscans displays the current text and normal overscan areas. Press the (Esc) key to exit this mode.

The Save gadget stores your changes to diskette. You should only do this on a copy of the Workbench diskette (not the original). The default filename is `oscan.prefs`. This file is located in the `prefs/env-archive` subdirectory. You can always save these to diskette later on in this session if you want to keep them.

The Use gadget tells the Amiga to use these changes, but does not save the changes to disk.

The Cancel gadget exits the Input program without saving or using any of the changes. The Workbench reappears with the original settings.

Palette

Palette allows you to adjust your colors by using the four boxes and three *sliders* in the window. Each color box matches a color on the screen. The sliders control the amount of red (R), green (G) and blue (B) in each color.

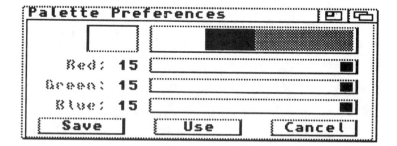

Palette Preferences Window

- Double-click the Palette icon.

- Click on the left hand color box. Look at the positions of the sliders.

The sliders change position as you click on each color box. These sliders show the degrees of red, green and blue in each color.

- Click on each of the color boxes, and look at the slider positions for each color box.

The sliders handle *primary colors*. The three primary colors are red, green and blue. Dragging the sliders left or right increases or decreases the amount of primary colors in the selected color.

- Click on the black color box.

- Move the pointer onto the box in the slider marked Blue, press and hold the left mouse button.

- Drag the blue slider all the way to the right.

The areas that were black change to blue. Note that the other two sliders remain to the far left.

- Move the pointer onto the box in the Green slider, press and hold the left mouse button.

- Drag the green slider all the way to the right.

The blue areas turn an aqua color.

- Move the pointer onto the box in the Red slider. Press and hold the left mouse button.

- Drag the red slider all the way to the right.

The aqua areas change to white. Also notice that any white text (for example, the icon names) now disappear.

- Drag the Blue slider all the way to the left.

The white areas change to yellow.

- Try the above color change procedures with all four color boxes.

- Click on the Cancel gadget.

The Cancel gadget returns any color changes to the colors loaded by the Workbench.

If you only wish to use the current color selections without saving them to diskette, select the Use gadget.

There are two ways you can change the colors back to their original settings:

1. Delete the file named palette.prefs located in the prefs/env-archive directory. This sets every change back to the Workbench settings as they were from the factory.

2. Dragging the sliders to their original positions.

The Save gadget will store your color information in the file named palette.prefs located in the prefs/env-archive directory. This color information is loaded each time you boot your Amiga.

The Use gadget tells the Amiga to use these changes but *does not* save the changes to disk.

The Cancel gadget exits the Input program without saving or using any of the changes. The Workbench reappears with the original settings.

Pointer

This Pointer program allows you to change the appearance of your mouse pointer. You'll use this program if you have your own ideas of the appearance and color of the mouse pointer.

• Double-click on the `Pointer` icon.

The `Pointer` window appears. In the middle of this window are four copies of the mouse pointer in normal size. A fifth pointer is magnified in the left side of the window.

• Move the pointer onto the small red box just between the RGB sliders and the Reset Color gadget. Click on the small red box. The box next to the four colors will change to red indicating the new drawing color.

• Click on the window containing the magnified pointer. Look at the magnified pointer window and the four duplicate windows to the right of the magnified view.

Note that a dot appears on each window at the location you clicked in the magnified view. This large window is where you edit your pointer.

• Click somewhere else in the background.

Each time you make a dot within the magnified window, a dot appears in the same location for each of the four smaller windows.

• Press and hold the left mouse button, and move the pointer around in the magnified view. Create a circle in the window.

• Release the left mouse button.

- Move the pointer onto the small black box just above the RGB sliders and click on it. The box next to the four colors will change to black indicating the new drawing color.

- Move the pointer into the magnified view.

- Press and hold the left mouse button, and move the pointer in a circular motion.

- Release the left mouse button.

The pointer now draws black dots instead of red ones. The circle you drew appears round in the smaller windows but it will appear more jagged in the magnified view. The many dots form lines and smoother shapes when you view them in normal size. Your current cursor remains unchanged until you click on the Use gadget.

- Press the right mouse button and select the Reset to defaults item in the **Edit** menu.

This changes the magnified pointer to its original form.

- Click on the Clear gadget.

This clears the magnified view except for the one dot in the upper left corner. This single dot is called the *point*. It marks that part of the mouse cursor which must be on the object for clicking or dragging.

You can move the point using the Set Point gadget.

- Click on the Set Point gadget.

- Move the pointer into the magnified view and click.

The point moves to the spot you clicked.

You can change colors of the pointer by using the sliders just as with changing colors in Palette. A box displays the active color. The Reset Color gadget restores the colors to the original colors.

The Save gadget stores your changes to diskette. You should only do this on a copy of the Workbench diskette (not the original). The default name is Pointer.pre in the prefs/env-archive directory. You can always save these to diskette later on in this session if you want to keep them.

The Use gadget tells the Amiga to use these changes, but does not save the changes to disk.

The Cancel gadget exits the Pointer program without saving or using any of the changes. The Workbench reappears with the original settings.

Printer
Editors

After switching on your printer and setting the DIP switches to the correct positions, switch on your Amiga.

Follow the instructions in your Amiga documentation for copying the printer driver(s) you need to the Devs/Printers drawer of your hard disk or boot diskette.

Workbench 2.0 includes two icons to control printer configuration: the Printer icon and the PrinterGfx icon. The Printer program lets you set the parameters that match the Amiga to your printer.

• Double click on the Printer icon.

After double-clicking on the Printer icon, the Printer Preferences window will appear.

This window contains a number of options for setting printer parameters. The Printer Driver scroll gadget lists the available printer drivers. Scroll through the list using the scroll arrows or scroll bar, and click on the name of the printer you're using.

The Amiga includes drivers for the following printers: Alphapro 101, Brother HR-15XL, CalComp Colormaster, CalComp Colormaster2, Cannon PJ1080A, CBM MPS-1000, Diabolo 630, Diabolo Advantage D25, Diabolo C-150, Epson FX/RX series, Howtek PixelMaster, HP DeskJet, HP LaserJet, HP PaintJet, Imagewriter II, Okidata 292, Okidata 92, Okimate 20, Quadram Quadjet, Qume Letterpro 20, Toshiba P351C, Toshiba P351SX and Xerox 4020. These drivers and

others may be on the Extras diskette, see the section CLI Tricks and Tips for more printer information.

- Click on the up arrow and down arrow in the top right of the Printer driver display window until you find the name of your printer.

- Click on your printer to select it or click the Cancel gadget to exit without changing printer parameters.

- If your printer does not appear on this list, try the EpsonQ setting and click on the OK gadget.

If the printer still doesn't work, contact your dealer. New printer drivers are available for many different printers.

If the printer is connected to the parallel port, click on the Printer Port: cycle gadget until it displays the word Parallel. If the serial port is used, click on the Printer Port: cycle gadget until it displays the word Serial.

Printer Port: 〔↕〕   Parallel

Printer Port
gadget

Unless you need to use a laser printer or your printer interface requires a serial port, the printer output port should remain set to Parallel. Very few printers use the serial port.

NOTE:

If you select Serial in the Printer Port: cycle gadget, you'll need to adjust the serial interface parameters from the Serial program, also included in the Prefs directory.

Click on the Paper Type: cycle gadget until it displays the proper paper type your printer currently uses (either Single or Fanfold).

Paper Type: 〔↕〕   Fanfold

Paper Type
gadget

Fanfold paper is also referred to as continuous form paper. It's perforated so you can separate the pages into normal size sheets. Single sheets are individual sheets such as a letterhead.

Click on the Paper Size: cycle gadget until it displays the paper size currently in use in your printer.

Paper Size: |C| U.S. Letter

Paper Size gadget

The following options are available:

- U.S. Letter   Standard letter size (8.5 x 11 inches).

- U.S. Legal   Legal size (8.5 x 14 inches).

- Narrow Tractor   Continuous form (9.5 x 11 inches).

- Wide Tractor   Continuous form (14.875 x 11 inches).

- Custom   Custom paper size as entered in the Paper Length (Lines):, Left Margin (Chars): and Right Margin (Chars): gadgets.

These choices are displayed each time you click on the gadget. If you select Custom, you must also specify the Length of the page (default of 66 lines).

Paper length allows you to set the size of the paper which you use for your printouts. The default is 66 lines.

Left Margin and Right Margin lets you adjust the margins. The numbers control the starting and ending columns of printed text. The only time you'll usually need to adjust this setting is when you use a type style smaller than the standard 10 characters per inch.

Print Pitch controls the pitch (the number of characters per inch). You can choose Elite (12 characters per inch), Fine (15 characters per inch) or Pica (10 characters per inch).

Print Pitch: |C| 10-Pica

Print Pitch gadget

When you click the gadget to select the pitch, make certain your printer supports that pitch. You may need to refer to your printer manual for that information.

Print Spacing gadget allows you to select the number of lines per inch (lpi). Changing this gadget affects the page length.

Print Spacing: [◆] 6 lpi

Print Spacing gadget

The following spacings are available:

6 lpi   Equivalent to standard typewriter spacing.

8 lpi   Almost 1.5 times as many lines per inch as 6 lpi.

The Amiga prints in two degrees of print quality as specified by the Print Quality gadget. Click on the Print Quality: cycle gadget until it displays the print quality you want. The Draft selection provides faster printing but lower quality. The Letter selection provides slower printing but higher quality.

Print Quality: [◆] Draft

Print Quality gadget

The Save gadget stores your changes to diskette. You should only do this on a copy of the Workbench diskette (not the original). The default filename is Printer.pre. You can always save these to diskette later on in this session if you want to keep them.

The Use gadget tells the Amiga to use these changes but *does not* save the changes to disk.

The Cancel gadget exits the Printer program without saving or using any of the changes. The Workbench reappears with the original settings.

Printergfx

Once you have completed the Printer Preferences, the screen returns to the Workbench. If you now need to fine-tune the graphics printing, open the PrinterGfx icon.

• Double click on the Printgfx icon.

The PrinterGfx Preferences window opens and displays the following screen:

```
┌──────────────────────────────────────────────────────────────┐
│ PrinterGfx Preferences                                  │⊡│⊏│ │
│      Color Correct          Smoothing         Left Offset      │
│   R: [  ] G: [  ] B: [  ]       [ ]        Inches / 10: [0]    │
│      [ Colors = 4096 ]                     Center Picture: [ ] │
│                                                                │
│   Dithering: [↻]   Ordered              Limits                 │
│   Scaling:   [↻]   Fraction        Type: [↻]   Ignore          │
│   Image:     [↻]   Positive        Width  (    ): [0░░░░░]     │
│   Aspect:    [↻]   Horizontal      Height (    ): [0░░░░░]     │
│   Shade:     [↻]   Black & White                               │
│                                                                │
│   Threshold: 7 [    ■    ]          Density:  1 [■       ]     │
│   [ Save ]              [ Use ]                    [ Cancel ]   │
└──────────────────────────────────────────────────────────────┘
```

PrinterGfx
Preferences
Window

This opens the `Printgfx` window. It displays the following gadgets:

Color
Correct
R/G/B

`Color Correct` tries to match the screen color to the colors available on the printer.

Color Correct

R: ☐ G: ☐ B: ☐
Colors = 4096

Color Correct
gadget

To select color correction, move the mouse pointer to the box next to the color you want to change. Press the left mouse button. A checkmark (√) appears in that box. You'll use all 4096 colors of the Amiga if you do not select color correct. However, for each color you select, 308 shades of that color are lost.

To test this on a color printer, create a picture with solid Red, Green and Blue colors. Then print this picture with different `Color Correct` settings and then without any color correction. The color corrected printout should appear more like the actual screen display.

Smoothing

When you switch on this gadget, the Amiga attempts to smooth diagonal lines on a printout to reduce their jagged appearance. You should select this gadget when using graphic dump programs. However, when smoothing is set the print speed will decrease.

*Left
Offset*

This gadget allows you to offset the picture from the left margin in increments of 1/10th of an inch.

Center

This gadget allows you to center the printed image. Centering takes precedence over a Left Offset.

Dithering

The Dithering: cycle gadget allows you to specify the type of dithering sent to the printer. Dithering performs some smoothing between shades of gray or between colors.

*Dithering
Cycle gadget*

The Amiga supports three types of dithering:

Ordered: where the shades are produced using an ordered pattern of dots.

Halftone: where the color intensity is calculated by the halftone method, which is similar to the technique used in printing newspapers and comic books. This method produces the best results with a printer that uses high print density (i.e., more than 150 dots per inch).

The Floyd-Steinburg error distribution method: where a dot pattern is created which maximizes the picture by distributing the intensities of each pixel and surrounding pixels. This form of dithering slows the printer speed in a 2:1 ratio because every dot is analyzed before it is printed.

If B&W Shading is selected in Shade, dithering is not performed.

Scaling

This gadget selects the scaling method. Fraction scaling is the default since it's normal scaling. The other option is the integer scaling where each dot on the screen will be an even number of printer dots.

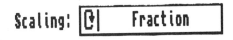

*Scaling
Cycle
gadget*

This may give a slight distortion to graphic pictures but is useful for printing fonts (bit-image text) so that they are not distorted by fractional scaling.

Image

The Image: cycle gadget controls the appearance of the printed image. (see the following figure). Click until this gadget displays Positive to print the image as it appears on the screen. Click until this gadget displays Negative to print black images as white and white images as black.

Aspect

The Aspect: cycle gadget specifies the aspect (orientation) of the printed page. The Horizontal setting prints graphics as they appear on the screen. The Vertical setting prints graphics at a 90 degree counterclockwise angle from the Horizontal setting.

Shade

The Shade: cycle gadget controls printer shading. The following types of shading are available:

Black & White   Shading in black and white (no greys).

Grey Scale 1   Shades of grey simulating color.

Grey Scale 2   Similar to Grey Scale 1, but supporting four shades of grey and the Amiga 2024 monitor (which supports 7 grey scales).

Color   Printing in color (color printers only).

Shade: |⟳| Black & White

Shade Cycle gadget

Black and White often provides a better printout than Gray Scale.

Threshold

The Threshold slider gadget specifies the amount of black and white contrast, and determines which colors are printed in black and which ones are printed in white. Dragging the slider changes the Threshold number. For example, if the Image: cycle gadget is set to Positive and the Threshold number is 1, only the darkest colors in the picture will be printed in black. By increasing the Threshold number, more colors will be printed in black.

$$\text{Threshold: 7}\ \boxed{\quad\quad\ \blacksquare\quad\quad\quad}$$

*Threshold
Cycle gadget*

If the Image gadget is set on Negative, however, then the lighter colors will be printed in black, according to the value set.

Limits

This gadget determines how the Amiga uses the values entered into the Width and Height Limits. Ignore ignores the limits. Bounded limits the printed pictures size by the limits you specify. Absolute uses the limit values as absolute values, the printed size is not bounded, its absolute size is specified. Pixels interprets the limit values as absolute printer pixels instead of tenths of an inch. Multiply will multiply the limits with the source pictures width and height.

*Width
Limit*

Limits the width of the printed picture in tenths of an inch, pixels or a multiplication factor.

*Height
Limit*

Limits the height of the printed picture in tenths of an inch, pixels or a multiplication factor.

Density

This gadget allows you to select different densities for graphic printouts. Different printers support different densities. The lower the density, the faster the printout.

The Save gadget stores your changes to diskette. You should only do this on a copy of the Workbench diskette (not the original). The default filename is PrinterGfx.pre. You can always save these to diskette later on in this session if you want to keep them.

The Use gadget tells the Amiga to use these changes but *does not* save the changes to disk.

The Cancel gadget exits the PrinterGfx program without saving or using any of the changes. The Workbench reappears with the original settings.

Serial

The Serial program sets parameters for data transfer through the serial port. Starting the Serial program opens a new window, containing gadgets named BAUD Rate, Input Buffer Size, Handshaking, Parity, Bits / Char, and Stop / Bits.

These settings depend entirely on the device performing the transfer (refer to the manual for information). Modems that allow data to be transferred over a telephone line are usually connected to the serial port. It depends on how you use your Amiga but usually you'll never need to use this window.

This is the rate at which data is transferred thru the serial port. The slowest rate is 110 (far left) and the fastest rate is 31250 (far right) using the slider.

```
┌─────────────────────────────────────────────────────────┐
│ Serial Preferences                                  ▣ ▣  │
│ ┌─────────────────────────────────────────────────────┐ │
│ │             BAUD Rate:   9600 [        ■         ]   │ │
│ │       Input Buffer Size:  512 [■                 ]   │ │
│ │                                                     │ │
│ │   Handshaking      Parity      Bits / Char  Stop Bits│ │
│ │   XON/XOFF ◉      None ◉         7 ○         1 ◉     │ │
│ │   RTS/CTS  ○      Even ○         8 ◉         2 ○     │ │
│ │   None     ○      Odd  ○                             │ │
│ │                   Mark ○                             │ │
│ │                   Space ○                            │ │
│ │   [ Save ]         [   Use   ]          [ Cancel ]   │ │
│ └─────────────────────────────────────────────────────┘ │
└─────────────────────────────────────────────────────────┘
```

Serial Preferences Window

BAUD Rate

Input Buffer Size

This is the size of the buffer used by the serial port. This is adjustable from 512 to 65536 using the slider gadget. The higher the setting the faster the transfer of data.

Hand-shaking

When computers or devices are connected together they must agree on a method of controlling the data flow between them. This gadget allows you to choose the correct method. The xON/xOFF software method is useful in modem communications. RTS/CTS is a hardware method (requires actual wires) and is useful for printers. RTS is an acronym for Request To Send and CTS is an acronym for Clear To Send.

Parity

Parity is a method of error checking when transmitting data. Your choices are Even, Odd or None.

Bits / Char

This is the actual size of data passed to the serial port. Early computers, like the Apple II could only use 7 bits, most computers today use 8 bits.

Stop Bits

Stops bits are extra bits at the end of a character. They inform the receiving computer or device (printer) of the proper spacing between words and the end of transmission.

Slower computers usually require 2 stop bits. Computers which operate at 300 baud or faster generally require 1 stop bit.

WBpattern

The WBpattern program allows you to edit the Workbench background pattern and the pattern used in other windows which display icons.

• Double click on the WBpattern program to open the window.

The open window displays the default pattern and the preset patterns. The current pattern is displayed magnified in the left of the WBpattern window. You can change the magnified pattern by using the mouse.

You can select the drawing colors by using the mouse to click on the color. This displays the active color above the colors. The edited pattern appears to the right of the colors.

The eight preset patterns appear below the display of the edited pattern. You can select these patterns by using the mouse pointer and pressing the left mouse button.

The Workbench gadget will use the current pattern in the Workbench window or screen. The Windows gadget uses the current pattern in windows displaying icons. Text display windows do not use a pattern. The Clear gadget clears the edited pattern. The Undo gadget restores your last edited pattern.

The Close gadget exits the program. The window size gadget reduces the window to only a title bar. The front/back gadget toggles the window from back to front.

Screen Mode

This allows you to select the mode for the screen display. The normal display modes are Lores, Hires, Lores-Interlaced, or Hires-Interlaced. If your Amiga has the Enhanced Amiga Chip Set you can access the new Productivity and SuperHires modes.

Other modes may also be available but depend on the configuration of your Amiga. These include the following modes: ntsc.monitor, pal.monitor, multisync.monitor, bisync.monitor and a 2024.monitor. The proprieties of the selected modes are displayed next to the display mode selections.

You can also choose the Width and Height of the screen. The Default is the size of the display, but you can enter larger values. The number of colors can range between 2 and 16. Since the screen can be larger than the display, Autoscroll can be turned on or off.

2.10   Preferences 1.3

One of the Workbench's most powerful features is Preferences. You can install and adjust most Amiga settings to your individual preference. Preferences is a single program in Workbench 1.3 Workbench 2.0 contains a drawer named Prefs containing individual programs. This is a flexible and important upgrade from Workbench 1.3.

Preferences consists of programs which are located in the Prefs drawer. We'll discuss Preferences 1.3 in this section (Workbench 2.0 users should refer to Section 2.9).

Workbench 1.3 Preferences

• Double-click the Prefs drawer icon in the Workbench window.

• Double-click the Preferences icon.

As soon as the program loads, a new window called Preferences appears. Note that this window has no close gadget or sizing gadget.

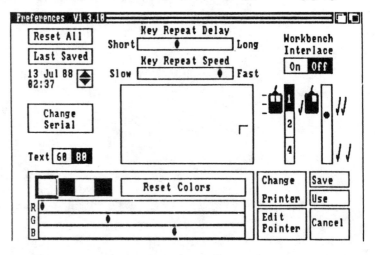

1.3 Preferences

• Move the pointer to the Preferences window drag bar. Press and hold the left mouse button.

• Try moving the window down.

You'll quickly discover that you cannot move the window and that it remains in the same location.

• Release the left mouse button.

- Look at the title bar as you press and release the right mouse button.

The Preferences window has no menu bar. The drag bar disappears when you press the right mouse button.

- Click on the back gadget of the Preferences window.

The Workbench window appears in front of the Preferences window. Also, any other windows remaining open also appear in front of the Preferences window.

The back and front gadgets of the Preferences window operate the same as back and front gadgets for other windows.

Date
Time

There are two gadgets toward the upper left corner of the Preferences window and below the Last Saved gadget. These gadgets let you set the current date and time.

The date gadget lists the day, month and year. A space separates each part of the date. The time gadget lists the hour and minute. A colon separates the hour and minute.

- Double-click the Clock icon in the Utilities window (click on the back and front gadgets if the Clock isn't currently open).

- Double-click on the Preferences icon (click on the back and front gadgets if Preferences isn't currently open).

- Move the pointer to the number you want changed in the Preferences window, and click on that number; the Amiga highlights that number for a moment.

- Click the up arrow to increase the number and the back arrow to decrease the number.

- Repeat the above two steps as needed for the other numbers (including the date).

- When you have the time correctly set, move the pointer to the lower right corner of the Preferences window and click on the Use gadget.

- Click on the Clock window to see the new date and time.

The clock time runs a few seconds later than the Preferences setting. Preferences uses the saved time setting as the starting time. If you start your Amiga every morning at eight o'clock, then you can set this time to 8:00. The Amiga clock then starts at eight o'clock every time you turn it on.

NOTE:

Time adjustments can affect both time and date. Moving the hour from 23 to 0 increases the day by one. Also, increasing the minutes from 59 to 0 increases the hour by one.

Moving the day up from 31 to 1 increases the month by one. For example, Jan changes to Feb. Also, increasing the month from Dec to Jan increases the year by one.

• Open the Preferences window.

• Follow the instructions above to change the time. Do not click the Use gadget after setting the time.

• Click the Preferences window's back gadget.

• Click on the Clock window and check the time.

The clock stays set at its old time. You must tell Preferences to use the changes.

• Click the Preferences window's front gadget.

Save
Use
Cancel

Note the three gadgets in the lower right corner of the Preferences window. The Cancel gadget cancels any changes made to Preferences in this session. The Save gadget saves your changes to diskette for later recall. The Use gadget tells the Amiga to use the current Preferences settings without saving them. These settings remain in effect until you switch off the Amiga.

• Click on the Use gadget.

The Preferences window disappears and the clock digits move to the time you set. The second counter begins at 00.

• Double-click the Preferences icon to reopen Preferences.

Here are the individual gadgets and settings available in Preferences.

Reset All

This gadget, in the upper right corner, returns all values in Preferences to the settings that originally came with your Workbench diskette. This is useful when you can't remember the original settings.

Last Saved

This gadget recalls the most recently saved settings. This is useful if you make an error and want the Preferences most recently saved to diskette.

Change
Serial

This gadget sets parameters for data transfer through the serial port. Selecting Change Serial opens a new window, containing gadgets named Baud Rate, Buffer Size, Read Bits, Write Bits, Stop Bits, Parity and Handshaking.

These settings depend entirely on the device performing the transfer (refer to the manual for information). Modems that allow data to be transferred over a telephone line are usually connected to the serial port. It depends on how you use your Amiga but usually you'll never need to use this window.

Baud Rate

This is the rate at which data is transferred thru the serial port. Use the arrow gadgets to change the settings. The range is 110 to 31250 with the higher setting representing the faster transfer rate.

Buffer size

This is the size of the buffer used by the serial port. Use the arrow gadgets to change the settings. The range is from 512 to 16000. A higher setting represents a faster transfer of data.

Read Write Bits

This is the actual size of data passed to the serial port. Early computers could only use 7 bits but more recent computers use 8 bits.

Stop Bits

Stop bits are extra bits at the end of a character. They inform the receiving computer or device (printer) of the proper spacing between words and the end of transmission.

Slower computers usually require 2 stop bits. Computers which operate at 300 baud or faster generally require 1 stop bit.

Parity

Parity is a method of error checking when transmitting data. Your choices are Even, Odd or None.

Even parity is an error-checking technique which sets an extra bit to 1 if the number of bits in a one byte data item adds up to an even number.

Odd parity is an error checking technique which sets an extra bit to 1 if the number of bits in a one byte data item adds up to an odd number.

Hand-shaking

Computers or devices which are connected together must agree on the method of controlling the data transfer between them. This gadget allows you to choose the correct method. The xON/xOFF software method is useful in modem communications. RTS/CTS is a hardware method (requiring actual wires) and is useful for printers. RTS is an acronym for Request To Send and CTS is an acronym for Clear To Send.

Text

This gadget determines the number of characters per line. The Text gadgets allow either 80 characters per line or 60 characters per line. Preferences highlights the active gadget in a different color. The Commodore RGB monitor works best with 80 characters per line. Other monitors read more clearly when the Amiga is set to 60 characters per line.

• Double-click the Preferences icon.

- Click on the opposite Text gadget number from the one currently set.

- Click on the Use gadget.

The character widths change on the screen.

- Double-click the Preferences icon.

- Click on the opposite text gadget number from the one currently set.

- Click on the Use gadget.

Workbench Colors

You will not find a gadget in the window with this name. Instead, you can adjust the screen colors by using the four boxes and three *sliders* across the bottom of the Preferences window. Each color box matches a color on the screen. The sliders control the amount of red (R), green (G) and blue (B) in each color.

- Double-click the Preferences icon.

- Click on the left hand color box. Look at the positions of the sliders.

The sliders change position as you click on each color box. These sliders show the degrees of red, green and blue in each color.

- Click on each of the color boxes. Look at the slider positions for each color box.

The sliders handle *primary colors*. The three primary colors are red, green and blue. You must drag the sliders left or right to increase or decrease the amount of primary colors in the selected color.

- Click on the black color box.

- Move the pointer onto the white dot in the blue slider (the slider marked B). Press and hold the left mouse button.

- Drag the blue slider all the way to the right.

The areas previously black now appear blue. Note that the other two sliders are all the way to the left.

- Click on the Reset Colors gadget.

The Reset Colors gadget returns any color changes to the colors loaded in by the Workbench.

- Move the pointer onto the white dot in the green slider (the slider marked G). Press and hold the left mouse button.

- Drag the green slider all the way to the right.

The black areas turn bright green.

- Move the pointer onto the white dot in the red slider (the slider marked R). Press and hold the left mouse button.

- Drag the red slider all the way to the right.

The green areas change to bright yellow.

- Drag the blue slider all the way to the right.

The yellow areas change to white. This also hides any white colored text.

- Click on Reset Colors.

- Try the above color change procedures with all four color boxes.

There are three ways to change colors back to their original settings:

1.   Clicking on the Reset Colors gadget.

2.   Clicking on the Reset All gadget. This sets every change back to the Workbench settings as they were from the factory.

3.   Dragging the sliders to their original positions.

Key Repeat Delay

This gadget adjusts the time delay between a key press and the key repeat. The Amiga waits for the amount of time you set here between your pressing a key and the first key repetition.

- Move the pointer onto the Key Repeat Delay slider.

- Press and hold the left mouse button.

- Drag the slider all the way to the left to Short.

- Click on the Preferences window's back gadget.

- Open the Utilities drawer and double-click on the Notepad icon.

- Press and hold a key for a second when the Notepad appears.

The key begins repeating almost immediately.

- Click on the Preferences window.

- Move the pointer onto the Key Repeat Delay slider.

- Press and hold the left mouse button.

- Drag the slider to the right until it is at Long.

- Click on the Notepad window.

- Press and hold a key until the key starts repeating.

The Amiga waits a second or two before it repeats the key.

Key Repeat Speed

This gadget adjusts the speed at which keys repeat when held down. For example, if you press and hold a key in the Notepad, the Amiga waits a moment then prints the letter until you release the key.

- Click on the Preferences window.

- Move the pointer onto the Key Repeat Speed slider.

- Press and hold the left mouse button.

- Drag the slider all the way to the right to Fast.

- Click on the Notepad window.

- Press and hold a key for a few seconds.

The Amiga prints the same letter on the Notepad a number of times, even after you release the key. The computer stores the number of key repeats in a *keyboard buffer*. This is an area in memory where keystrokes are stored before the Amiga uses them. After you release the key, the Amiga continues printing the repeated letter until this buffer empties.

- Drag any windows out of the way of the Preferences window's Key Repeat Speed slider.

- Move the pointer onto the Key Repeat Speed slider.

- Press and hold the left mouse button.

- Drag the slider all the way to the left to Slow.

- Click on the Notepad window.

- Press and hold a key for five or more seconds.

The letters repeat very slowly.

- Click on the Reset All gadget to restore the original settings.

Display Centering

This area has no gadget name. Dragging the corner shaped character moves the upper left corner of the screen.

- Move the pointer onto the corner shaped character in the center box of the Preferences window.

- Press and hold the left mouse button and drag the corner shaped character.

The corner shaped character moves, and so does the entire screen.

Workbench
Interlace

These gadgets set *interlace mode* on or off. Interlace mode is the Amiga's special setting for high-resolution graphics. This mode only works with very high quality monitors; most monitors show a jittery picture. You may never need this mode, but if you would like to see it:

- Click on the On gadget for Workbench Interlace.

- Click on the Save gadget.

- When the disk drive stops, hold down the Ctrl key and press the <Commodore logo> (or left <Amiga>) and right <Amiga> keys at the same time (this will reset the Amiga).

Watch the screen display.

- After the Workbench has loaded, double-click the Workbench disk icon.

- Double-click on the Prefs drawer (if available).

- Double-click the Preferences icon.

- Click on the Off gadget for Workbench Interlace.

- Click on the Save gadget.

- When the disk drive stops, hold down the Ctrl key and press the <Commodore logo> (or left <Amiga>) and right <Amiga> keys at the same time.

- Open the Workbench window by double clicking on the Workbench icon.

- Double-click on the Prefs drawer, if available.

- Double-click on the Preference icon.

Mouse
Speed

This area has no gadget name. It sets the mouse pointer speed. Each number (1, 2 or 4) represents the number of inches of mouse movement to move the pointer one third of a screen.

- Move the pointer onto the Mouse Speed gadget (the vertical bar with the numbers 1, 2 and 4 displayed in it).

- Click on the 4 gadget and move the pointer around.

The 4 setting makes the pointer move very slowly.

- Move the pointer onto the Mouse Speed gadget.

- Click on the 1 gadget and move the pointer around.

- Click on the Reset All gadget.

*Double
Click
Delay*

This has no gadget name. It sets the time delay allowed between the first and second clicks of a double-click. It lets you adjust the time between the first click and the second click of a double-click.

- Move the pointer onto the Double-Click Delay gadget (the vertical slider with checkmarks next to it) and press and hold the left mouse button.

- Drag the slider to the bottom.

- Click on the Utilities window.

- Click once on the Calculator icon, wait a few seconds, and click again.

The bottom setting allows up to a four second delay between the first and second click.

- Close the Calculator by clicking on its close gadget.

- Move the pointer onto the Double-Click Delay gadget.

- Drag the slider to the top.

*Change
Printer*

This item lets you set the parameters that match the Amiga to your printer. You can also access it by double-clicking on the Printer icon in the Prefs drawer (1.3 only).

- Click on the Change Printer gadget.

The Change Printer screen opens. This window contains a number of options for setting printer parameters. Workbench 1.2 did not include the Graphic 2 option (we'll discuss these parameters below).

*Amiga printer
support*

The Amiga includes drivers for the following printers: Alphapro 101, Brother HR-15XL, CBM MPS-1000, Diabolo 630, Diabolo Advantage D25, Diabolo C-150, Epson FX/RX series, Epson JX-80, HP LaserJet, HP LaserJet Plus, Okidata 292, Okidata 92, Okimate 20 and Qume Letterpro 20. There is also a generic printer setting. These drivers and others may be on the Extras diskette, see Section 4.3, CLI Tricks and Tips for more printer information.

- Click on the up arrow and down arrow in the top center of the Change Printer screen until you find the name of your printer.

- Click the OK gadget when your printer appears in the upper right window in highlighted text, or click the Cancel gadget to exit without changing printer parameters.

- If you own a printer not on the list, try the generic printer or Epson setting and click on the OK gadget.

If the printer still doesn't work see your dealer, new printer drivers are available for many different printers.

The Change Printer screen contains the following printer parameter options:

Parallel/ Serial

Click the printer icon for parallel printer output, or the telephone icon for serial printer output. Unless you have a laser printer, or your printer interface requires a serial port, the printer output port can stay set to Parallel. Very few printers use the serial port.

Printer Type

Click the up arrow and the down arrow to look through the list of printers. The printer marked for selection appears in highlighted type in the center of this window. Custom is the name chosen for a custom printer.

Paper Size/ Length

There are five paper sizes supported by the Amiga: U.S. Letter (8 1/2" x 11"), U.S. Legal (8 1/2" x 14"), Narrow Tractor (9 1/2" x 11"), Wide Tractor (14 7/8" x 11") and Custom. If you select Custom, you must also specify the Length of the page (default of 66 lines).

Paper Type

The Amiga accepts two types of paper: Single and Fanfold. Fanfold paper is also referred to as continuous form paper. It's perforated so you can separate it into normal size sheets. Single sheets are individual sheets such as letterhead paper.

Quality

The Amiga prints in two degrees of quality: Draft (low-quality) and Letter (high-quality).

Left/ Right Margin

This area lets you adjust the margins. The numbers control the starting and ending columns of printed matter. Usually this setting will only need adjustment if you work with a type style smaller than the standard 10 characters per inch.

Pitch

This controls the character size. You can choose Elite (12 characters per inch), Fine (15 characters per inch) or Pica (10 characters per inch). Click the desired field to select the pitch, if your printer supports that pitch. See your printer manual for that information.

Spacing

This controls the spacing of lines on the page. Select either the 6 lpi (lines per inch) or 8 lpi gadget.

Graphic 1

This gadget opens the Graphic 1 screen, which allows you to fine-tune the graphics printing. Graphic Select appears here in Workbench 1.2 and Workbench 1.3 added Graphic 2 for extra fine tuning control.

• Click on the Graphic 1 gadget.

The Graphic 1 screen opens. It contains the following gadgets:

Threshold

This determines which colors are printed as black or white. More colors are printed as black the farther right you position the controller. Usually the default setting of two works quite well. Dragging the triangle positioned above the number bar changes the Threshold setting.

Aspect

This gadget sets either horizontal or vertical printing.

Shade

Sets the printer shading for Black and White, Gray Scale (shades of gray simulating color), Gray Scale 2 (for screens designed on the Amiga 2024 monitor, which supports 7 gray scales) or Color printing (if your printer prints in color). Black and White often gives a better printout than Gray Scale.

Image

Prints a hardcopy as Positive (black is black and white is white) or Negative (white becomes black and black becomes white).

• Click on the OK gadget to accept new values, or the Cancel gadget to exit without changes. Either gadget returns you to the Change Printer screen.

• Click on the OK gadget of the Change Printer screen to accept new values, or the Cancel gadget to exit. Either gadget returns you to the Preferences window.

Graphic 2

This gadget opens the Graphic 2 screen, which allows further fine-tuning when printing graphics. This was not available in Workbench 1.2.

• Click on the Graphic 2 gadget.

The Graphic 2 screen opens. It contains the following gadgets:

Smoothing

Sometimes a diagonal line will appear jagged on a printout. When you switch on this gadget, the Amiga attempts to smooth diagonal lines on a printout to reduce the jagged appearance.

Left Offset

This gadget allows you to offset the picture from the left margin in 1/10th inch increments.

Center

This gadget allows you to center the printed image. Centering takes precedence over a Left Offset.

Density

This gadget allows you to select different densities for graphic printouts. Different printers support different densities. The lower the density, the faster the printout.

Color Correct R/G/B

Color correction tries to match the screen color to the colors available on the printer.

To select color correction, move the mouse pointer to the box next to the color you want to change. Press the left mouse button. The box changes color to indicate that you selected it. You'll use all 4096 colors of the Amiga if you do not select color correct. However, for each color you select, you'll lose 308 shades of that color.

To test this on a color printer, create a picture with solid Red, Green and Blue colors. Then print this picture with different Color Correct settings and then without any color correction. The color corrected printout should appear more like the actual screen display.

Dithering

This gadget sets the dithering mode. Dithering is the process of printing several different colored dots so they're smaller and closer together. This makes these dots appear as one color.

The Amiga supports three types of dithering. If you select Ordered, the shades are produced using an ordered pattern of dots. Halftone changes the size and density of the dots to form the color intensities. This method is similar to newsprint. The third is the Floyd-Steinburg error distribution method where a dot pattern is created which maximizes the picture by distributing the intensities of each pixel and surrounding pixels. Selecting the Floyd-Steinburg error distribution method may decrease the speed of your printer.

Scaling

This gadget selects the scaling method. Fractional scaling is normal, with integer scaling each dot on the screen will be an even number of printer dots. This may give a slight distortion to graphic pictures but is useful for printing fonts so that they are not distorted by fractional scaling.

Width Limit

Limits the width of the printed picture in tenths of an inch, pixels or a multiplication factor.

Height Limit

Limits the height of the printed picture in tenths of an inch, pixels or a multiplication factor.

<- Limits

This gadget determines how the values entered into the Width and Height Limits are used. Ignore ignores the limits. Bounded limits the size of the printed picture by the limits you enter. Absolute uses the limit values as absolute values, the printed size is not bounded, its absolute size is specified. Pixels interprets the limit values as absolute printer pixels instead of tenths of an inch. Multiply will multiply the limits with the width and height of the source picture.

- Click on the OK gadget to accept new values, or the Cancel gadget to exit without changes. Either gadget returns you to the Change Printer screen.

- Click on the OK gadget of the Change Printer screen to accept new values, or the Cancel gadget to exit. Either gadget returns you to the Preferences window.

Edit
Pointer

This Pointer program allows you to change the appearance of your mouse pointer. You'll use this program if you have your own ideas of the appearance and color of the mouse pointer.

- Double-click on the Pointer icon.

The Pointer window appears. In the middle of this window are four copies of the mouse pointer in normal size. A fifth pointer is magnified in the left side of the window.

- Click on the magnified pointer window's blue background. Look at the magnified pointer window, and the four duplicate windows to the right of the magnified view.

- Click on the window containing the magnified pointer. Look at the magnified pointer window and the four duplicate windows to the right of the magnified view.

Note that a dot appears on each window at the location you clicked in the magnified view. This large window is where you edit your pointer.

- Click somewhere else in the background.

Each time you make a dot within the magnified window, a dot appears in the same location for each of the four smaller windows.

- Press and hold the left mouse button. Move the pointer around in the magnified view. Make the window as messy as you can.

- Release the left mouse button.

- Move the pointer onto the small black box just above the RGB sliders and click on it.

The sliders all move as far left as they can go. Also, a border appears around the black box. This indicates that black is the active color.

- Move the pointer into the magnified view.

- Press and hold the left mouse button, and move the pointer in a circular motion.

- Release the left mouse button.

The pointer now draws black dots instead of red ones. The circle you drew appears round in the smaller windows but it will appear more jagged in the magnified view. The many dots form lines and smoother shapes when you view them in normal size. Your current cursor remains unchanged until you click on the OK gadget.

- Click on the Restore gadget.

This gadget changes the magnified pointer to its original form.

- Click on the Clear gadget.

This clears the magnified view except for the one dot in the upper left corner. This single dot is called the *point*. It marks that part of the mouse cursor which must be on the object for clicking or dragging.

You can move the point using the Set Point gadget.

- Click on the Set Point gadget.

- Move the pointer into the magnified view and click.

The point reappears at the spot you clicked.

Change colors using the sliders, the same way that you changed colors in Preferences. A border surrounds the currently active color.

Clicking the OK gadget returns you to Preferences window. If you make a mistake with the mouse, you can still fix it from Preferences by selecting the Reset All gadget.

- Draw in the magnified view—make the pointer as messy as you can.

- Click on the OK gadget to return to Preferences.

- Click on the Reset All gadget.

The pointer returns to its original appearance.

Save This gadget stores your changes to diskette. You should only do this on a copy of the Workbench diskette (not the original).

Use This gadget tells the Amiga to use these changes until you change them again or switch off your Amiga. You can always save these to diskette later on in this session if you want to keep them.

Cancel This exits Preferences without saving or using any of the changes. The Workbench screen reappears with original settings.

2.11   Other Workbench tools

Workbench 2.0 has four menu titles, `Workbench`, `Window`, `Icons` and `Tools`. Workbench 1.3 has three menu titles: `Workbench`, `Disk` and `Special`. Although we discussed many of their functions in the preceding sections, some items require an additional explanation.

Also, we need to define a few things not on the menu. We'll first discuss Workbench 2.0 and then we'll explain the Workbench 1.3 method.

Reset

The last section demonstrated a *reset*. A reset is almost like switching the power to the computer off and on. This not only resets all values but it also clears memory.

Make sure that you're using a <u>copy</u> of the Workbench diskette in the internal drive, that all data is saved and that the disk drive LED is OFF before trying this procedure.

WARNING:

Never reset the Amiga while the disk drive is running. This could destroy data on the diskette.

- Press and hold the `Ctrl` key.

- Press and hold the <Commodore logo> (or left <Amiga>) key.

- Press the right <Amiga> key.

The screen goes blank, the drive runs and the Workbench screen reappears. You can then restart the Amiga whenever you want.

At first sight your Workbench screen looks exactly as it always did. However, the name of the diskette icon says `Copy Of Workbench`, not `Workbench`. If it only says `Workbench`, you're still using the original diskette. Make a backup before you do anything else (see The System drawer section for information on copying diskettes).

- Double-click the `Copy Of Workbench` diskette icon.

More Workbench

A window appears containing all the visible icons. Unlike the original Workbench diskette, you can save changes and programs to this diskette.

- Press and hold the right mouse button.

- Move the pointer onto the **Windows** menu title. Workbench 1.3 users should move the pointer onto the **Workbench** menu title.

- Select the `Close` item from the **Windows** pulldown menu. Workbench 1.3 users should select the `Close` item from the **Workbench** pulldown menu.

The **Workbench** window disappears.

Open/
Close

As mentioned previously, `Open` is an alternate method of opening files and icons. The `Close` item is an alternate method of closing files and icons.

- Click once on the `Workbench` diskette icon.

- Press and hold the right mouse button.

- Move the pointer onto the **Icons** menu title. Workbench 1.3 users should move the pointer onto the **Workbench** menu title.

- Select the `Open` item.

Copy or
Duplicate

The `Copy` (`Duplicate` in 1.3) item in the **Icons** menu (**Workbench** in 1.3) copies files, drawers and entire diskettes. Before using this item, make sure the destination diskette has sufficient free memory.

- Click once on the `Expansion` drawer icon.

- Press and hold the right mouse button.

- Move the pointer onto the **Icons** menu title. Workbench 1.3 users should move the pointer onto the **Workbench** menu title.

- Select the `Copy` item from the **Icons** pulldown menu. Workbench 1.3 users should select the `Duplicate` item from the **Workbench** pulldown menu.

In a moment an icon named `copy_of_Expansion` appears on the screen. Note the underline characters between the words in the name. This is new in Workbench 2.0. The spaces used in Workbench 1.3 were easy to read but were difficult to access the drawer.

Workbench 2.0 users must make some room on the diskette to preform the next steps. MAKE SURE YOU ARE WORKING WITH A COPY OF YOUR WORKBENCH DISKETTE AND NOT THE ORIGINAL! Select the `WBstartup` drawer with the mouse. Next select `Delete...` from the **Icons** menu. Then confirm the deletion in the requester. You now should have enough free diskette space to continue.

- Duplicate `copy_of_Expansion` following the above steps.

The copy of the copy receives the name `copy_2_of_Expansion`. Use the mouse and pointer to enlarge the window (or use the scroll bars) if necessary to view the new drawer.

If you want to make more than two backup copies, you should make each from the most recent copy.

Rename

You may prefer to change the name `copy_2_of_Expansion` to something else. Use the `Rename` item for this.

- Click on the `copy_2_of_Expansion` icon.

- Select the `Rename` item from the **Icons** pulldown menu. Workbench 1.3 users should select the `Rename` item from the **Workbench** pulldown menu.

A requester appears on the screen when you select this item. This requester contains a string gadget listing the name `copy_2_of_Expansion`.

- Workbench 1.3 users will have to click on the string gadget. Another improvement in Workbench 2.0 is that it automatically activates the requester.

- Press the ⬅ (Backspace) key until the old name disappears.

- Type in the new name `Nothing` for the drawer.

Only letters to the right of the cursor can be deleted with the ⬚Del⬚ key. The ⬅ (Backspace) key deletes letters to the left of the cursor. If you make a mistake, you can delete with these two keys. Also, if you want to erase the name completely in the window, use the right <Amiga> ⬚X⬚ key combination.

Use the ⬅ and ➡ keys to move the cursor inside the string gadget. The cursor keys will not delete any characters or spaces.

- Press the ⬚⬅⬚ key.

You'll hear the disk drives operate as the Amiga changes the name of the disk. In a moment, the new name appears under the `Copy_2_of_Expansion` icon. You can change the name of any icon with the `Rename` item regardless if the object is a tool, project or diskette icon.

Information

The `Information` item of the **Icons** menu allows you to read and insert all sorts of information on icons and programs. Workbench 1.3 users use the `Info` item in the **Workbench** menu.

- Open the `Utilities` drawer.

- Click on the `Clock` icon.

•   Press and hold the right mouse button.

•   Select the `Info` item from the **Icons** menu. Workbench 1.3 users should select the `Info` item from the **Workbench** menu.

The `Information` window appears for this icon. The window displays the name of the program and its type (in this case, a `Tool`). The `Information` window also lists the `size` of the appropriate program. This file is 20224 bytes, or 42 *blocks*, long. The size of your clock size may differ (see the Appendices for a definition of block).

The last item is the `Stack` information. Since this item is seldom accessed by most users, <u>don't</u> <u>touch it</u> now. A wrong setup now may lead to several serious problems. Unfortunately, the solution to most of these problems is a system reset.

The status of a file is also listed. Since an `Archived` file was backed up, this has made an archival copy. You can throw away a `Deletable` file. Workbench 2.0 also includes `Script` and `Pure` status gadgets. For more information on the script and pure bit status flags, refer to the section on AmigaDOS.

Workbench 1.3 also included a status gadget for either `READABLE/WRITEABLE` or `NOT READABLE/WRITEABLE`. Although you could change this status with the mouse, normally you would not need or want to change it.

The programs that you use on the Amiga will alter the status of certain files. Workbench 2.0 allows you to change this status thru the Shell. For more information on the Shell, refer to the section on AmigaDOS.

Workbench 2.0 displays the date you last changed the file. This allows you to see the creation date of a file or the date you last edited the file.

Another gadget in these `Information` windows has the name `Comment`. Here you can enter any type of note you need for small reminders on a subject.

•   Click on `Comment`.

•   Type in `The Timekeeper` and press the ⏎ key.

The Shell icon and other project icons display another gadget called the Default Tool. This gadget allows the icon to call another tool and adds to the flexibility of the Amiga's operating system.

The `Tool Types` gadget is used to insert important information about default window sizes, fonts and other important operating system information that a program may require. Although you could change the information present in `Tool Types` by using the mouse, normally you would not need or want to change it. The programs that you use on the Amiga will keep track of this information.

Notice the Save gadget and a Quit gadget. Selecting Save stores all changes to the Information window. Selecting Quit exits the window without making changes. The third method of exiting the Information window is the Close gadget.

- Click on the Close gadget of the Information window.

The normal Workbench screen should now reappear. If you select Information for one of the drawers, the type is Drawer.

- Select the Utilities drawer.

- Press and hold the right mouse button.

- Select the Info item from the **Icons** menu. Workbench 1.3 users should select the Info item from the **Workbench** menu.

Notice the differences between the two Information windows. A drawer Information window has the type drawer and does not display any size information.

Delete
Discard

The Delete (Discard in 1.3) item performs the same task as the Trashcan icon.

- Activate the copy of Expansion that you renamed Nothing.

- Select the Delete item from the **Icons** pulldown menu. Workbench 1.3 users should select the Discard item from the **Workbench** pulldown menu.

A requester similar to the following appears:

Delete
Warning:

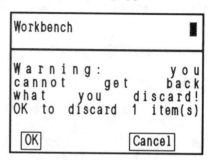

Be careful using the Delete function. You cannot undo the Delete function. If you accidentally select Delete, click on the Cancel gadget. Workbench 1.3 users should select the forget it! gadget.

• Click on the ok to discard gadget to proceed.

After the icon disappears, note that the free space on the disk increases. On Workbench 1.3 note the slight drop in the disk gauge on the left of the window.

There is still a copy_of_Expansion in the **Workbench** diskette window. Here's a different way to move icons.

• Drag the copy_of_Expansion icon outside the **Workbench** diskette window.

• Place it somewhere on the Workbench.

The copy_of_Expansion disappears from the **Workbench** diskette window and reappears somewhere on the Workbench.

• Close the **Workbench** diskette window.

The copy_of_Expansion stays on the Workbench.

• Double-click copy_of_Expansion.

You can remove files, programs or other items from their windows and open them outside the windows. This is a practical and useful feature.

For example, say you frequently use the CLOCK but find the procedure of opening the Utilities drawer every time to open CLOCK is too time consuming. Instead, open the Utilities drawer once, drag the CLOCK onto the Workbench, and you'll no longer need to open the Utilities drawer to open CLOCK.

Another advantage to movable icons is easy file copying.

WARNING: Single drive Amiga owners must exchange diskettes often when copying. Remember to remove diskettes from the drive only when the disk drive LED is off. Even if the requester appears prompting you to remove a diskette from the drive, make sure that all the drive operations have finished. **Never take a diskette out of a drive while the drive is in operation.**

• Insert a formatted diskette into your drive.

A disk icon appears on the Workbench named Empty.

• Drag copy_of_Expansion drawer onto the Empty disk icon.

Single drive Amiga owners are requested to insert your Workbench diskette.

- Insert the requested diskette.

The Amiga now gets the necessary information from copy_of_Expansion on your Workbench. A hint for those with two drives: Simply insert the Empty diskette into the second drive and drag the copy_of_Expansion icon onto the Empty disk icon.

Single drive users

Read and remember the above warning when copying diskettes. Ignoring this warning may destroy the data on your Empty diskette. Once the copy procedure is complete, take a look at the Empty diskette window.

- Open the Empty diskette icon.

The copy_of_Expansion icon just copied should appear somewhere in the window. The original copy_of_Expansion still appears on the Workbench screen because it was only copied and not moved.

You can also move icons from one window to another.

- Open the Workbench diskette window by double clicking on the Workbench diskette icon.

- Open the Utilities drawer in the Workbench diskette window.

- Open the Expansion drawer in the Workbench diskette window.

If the Workbench diskette is not in the drive, the Amiga requests it.

- Drag the Clock icon from the Utilities window into the Expansion window.

Soon after the disk drive finishes its work, the Clock icon disappears from the Utilities window and reappears in the Expansion window. The Clock icon also disappears when you close the Expansion window.

- Drag the Clock icon back into the Utilities window.

When you drag an icon from one diskette window into another diskette window, the Amiga copies the program and icon. You may now have several copies_of_Expansion. It's time to delete a few of these.

- Take a copy_of_Expansion.

- Drag it onto the Trashcan icon.

Make sure that the Trashcan icon is in the same diskette window as the copy_of_Expansion. This means that if you want to delete an icon from the Workbench diskette window, then you must place this icon onto the Trashcan in the Workbench diskette window.

• Select the Trashcan icon to activate it

• Select Empty Trash from the **Icons** pulldown menu. Workbench 1.3 users should select Empty Trash from the **Disk** pulldown menu.

Empty
Trash

Soon after the disk drive finishes its work, the copy_of_Expansion disappears. The Trashcan temporarily stores the file in another area of the diskette and before you discard the file using the Empty Trash item from the Icons (**Disk** 1.3) menu (see Section 2.8).

RAM disk

The Amiga 500 Workbench produces a diskette icon named RAM disk. This icon acts like a normal floppy diskette but with these differences:

1. It's much faster than floppy or hard diskettes.

2. It's temporary; anything saved or copied to the RAM disk disappears once you switch off the Amiga. To keep the data in the RAM disk, you must save contents of the RAM disk to a floppy diskette or hard disk.

3. You cannot format a RAM disk.

4. RAM disk capacity is small compared to floppy diskettes (unless you have expanded memory).

• Drag the Clock icon from the Utilities window to the RAM disk icon.

• Double-click on the RAM disk icon.

• Double-click the Clock icon in the RAM disk icon.

See how quickly the RAM disk opens the window and starts the Clock; much faster than normal diskettes.

Also notice the memory bar on the top of the **RAM disk**. It always displays 100% full and OK free.

• Drag the entire Utilities drawer from the **Workbench** diskette window to the **RAM disk** window.

• Watch the memory bar on the top of the Workbench screen.

The RAM disk is still full, but the Utilities drawer is copied to the RAM disk. The Amiga's RAM disk is always full and is dependent on the computer's memory. Therefore, the RAM disk is *virtual*. *RAM* (Random Access Memory), the memory used for your programs and working space, provides as much available space as is required for the RAM disk.

There is a disadvantage to the RAM disk, however. The more memory occupied by the RAM disk, the slower programs run.

Remember that although the RAM disk is extremely fast, it takes up large amounts of RAM. Unless you have memory expansion built into the Amiga, use the RAM disk sparingly.

We do recommend using the RAM disk when copying diskettes on a single-disk system. Using the RAM disk this way avoids the constant diskette changing.

2.12   The Workbench Menus

In this section we'll discuss in detail the complete individual menus of Workbench 2.0 as they appear on the screen. In the following section we'll discuss the Workbench 1.3 menus.

Workbench 2.0 menus

Workbench	Window	Icons	Tools
Backdrop	New drawer	Open	ResetWB
Execute Command	Open Parent	Copy	
Redraw All	Close	Rename	
Update All	Update	Information	
Last Error	Select Contents	Snapshot	
Version	Clean up	UnSnapshot	
Quit	Snapshot	Leave Out	
	Show	Put Away	
	View		
		Delete	
		Format Disk	
		Empty Trash	

Workbench menu

The Workbench menu consists of the following items:

Backdrop   Switches the Workbench from a window to a screen. You can place a window on a screen but you cannot place a screen in a window. This is a major improvement over Workbench 1.3 which only allowed a Workbench screen.

• Select Backdrop from the **Workbench** menu.

The Workbench window disappears and the diskette icons are placed directly on a Workbench screen. The difference between a screen and a window is that it cannot be sized and windows are placed on a screen. This screen becomes the background, or backdrop, for all other windows. The front/back gadgets will not place their windows on the backdrop. Since a window is more flexible than a screen, return the Workbench back to a Workbench window:

• Select Backdrop from the **Workbench** menu.

Now you can access the Workbench through the Workbench window.

Execute Command

This menu item allows you to execute any AmigaDOS command without opening the Shell window. We'll discuss the different AmigaDOS commands in Chapter 4.

A requester appears which prompts you to enter the name of the AmigaDOS command and its arguments. Arguments are additional items or variables.

After entering the command, select the OK gadget or press the ⊕ key. Select Cancel if you do not want to execute the command.

Redraw All

Sometimes programs will disrupt a part of the screen. When this occurs select **Redraw all** from the **Workbench** pulldown menu. This item restores the open windows to their original appearance. This is one of the few Amiga items which you can access any time.

- Open a few diskette icons and drawer icons. Next select **Redraw All** from the **Workbench** menu.

The windows on the Workbench flash and their displays are updated from memory.

Update All

This item is helpful when you use Shell and the Workbench extensive. The difference between this item and Redraw All is that Update All updates the Workbench memory by re-reading information from the diskette. The original screen is redrawn from the updated memory. This is one of the few Amiga items which you can access any time.

- Open a few diskette icons and drawer icons. Next select Update All from the **Workbench** menu.

The windows on the Workbench are cleared and their displays are updated from information read from the diskette.

Last Error

This item redisplays the last error detected by the Amiga. There is no error when this item appears in ghost print.

The following is an intentional error to demonstrate this item:

- Drag the Workbench diskette icon up to the top of the Workbench screen.

Notice the screen flashes and the Workbench diskette icon reappears at its previous location. The title bar displays the Icons cannot be moved into this window error message.

- Click somewhere on the Workbench screen.

The message disappears. Suppose you didn't see that error message, and wanted to know what it said:

- Select Last Error from the **Workbench** pulldown menu.

The error message reappears on the title bar. It will reappear each time you select Last Error. The message changes when another error occurs.

Other common error messages include:

disk write-protected

disk full

object not found

Version Displays the current Workbench and Kickstart version numbers on the top line of the Workbench.

- Select the Version item from the **Workbench** pulldown menu.

Version numbers of the Workbench change as the developers of the Amiga improve the Workbench programming. There should be no problem as long as your version number is 33.56 or higher.

Quit Select this item if you want to close the Workbench program and its operations. Usually you will not select this item unless a program you are running becomes very low on memory.

All Workbench windows must be closed before you can select Quit. An error message will appear in the title bar informing you that a "wb program(s) is launched". Although you must close any open windows, drawers and disks can remain open.

This item removes the Workbench program from memory and frees up memory but also removes the Workbench user interface.

A requester appears to confirm that you want to close the Workbench window. Select the OK gadget to continue or CANCEL to return to the Workbench.

Window

You can open the Window menu only when you select a window. All of the items affect only the active window. Its border has a different color than the other windows.

New Drawer

This is a new Workbench item. It creates an `Empty` drawer in the current diskette window. Workbench 1.3 required you to have an `Empty` drawer file on each diskette. You had to copy this `Empty` drawer file each time to create a new drawer.

To open a new drawer:

* Open the `RAM Disk` icon by double clicking on it.

* Select `New drawer` from the Windows menu.

A new drawer name `Unnamed` is created on the active diskette. If you choose `New drawer` again the next drawer will be named `Unnamed2`. You can use the `Delete` item in the **Icons** menu to delete the drawer.

Open Parent

This option allows you to quickly locate the parent diskette of an opened drawer. This is extremely useful when drawers contain other drawers or you are working with multiple diskettes.

* Open the `Utilities` drawer on the `Workbench` diskette by double clicking on it.

* Close the `Workbench` diskette by clicking on the close gadget.

* Activate the `Utilities` window by clicking the mouse pointer inside it.

* Select `Open parent` from the **Windows** menu.

The Workbench diskette opens as the parent directory in this case. It's also possible for the parent to be a drawer when drawers contain other drawers.

Close

Closes the current window. This is the same as clicking on the close gadget in the upper left corner of a window.

Update

Updates the display of the active window from disk. Although `Update` is similar to `Update All`, it only updates the active window.

Select Contents

Selects the entire contents of an active window for easy file copying and deletion.

* Double-click the `Workbench` diskette icon.

* Select `Select Contents` from the **Windows** menu.

Now the entire contents in the active window is selected.

Clean Up   This item puts icons in a selected drawer or diskette into a proper and
clear order.

- Double-click the Workbench diskette icon.

- Double-click the System drawer to open it.

- Drag a few icons to different places in the System window.

- Click on the System window to make sure it is the active
  window.

- Select the **Window** pulldown menu.

- Select the Clean Up item, and watch the System window.

The Amiga automatically tidies up the System window. You can also
clean up entire diskettes:

- Double-click the Workbench diskette icon.

- Make the Workbench window very disorganized by dragging a
  few icons to scattered locations in the window.

- Click once on the Workbench window to activate it.

- Select the Window pulldown menu.

- Select the Clean Up item and watch the Workbench window.

Remember that Clean Up works only on active windows. This is
different than Workbench 1.3 which worked on diskette and drawer
icons and not on windows.

Snapshot   This function has two submenu items. When the Snapshot item is
selected the submenu items will be displayed in a menu next to the
pulldown menu. The first sub item is Window. It stores the position
and size of the active window. The second sub item is Contents. It
stores the order of icons in the active window.

Snapshot allows you to determine the positions of the individual
icons within a window as well as the window size and the point on the
screen at which it appears.

- Open the Workbench diskette window by double clicking on its
  icon.

- Reduce the size of the Workbench diskette window as much as
  possible using the sizing gadget.

- Select the submenu item Window diskette from the Snapshot
  item of the **Windows** menu.

- Close the Workbench diskette window by double clicking on it.

- Open the Workbench diskette window by double clicking on its icon.

Snapshot Window ensures that the window reopens at the size and location at which you set the window when you selected Snapshot Window.

Snapshot can also be used to record the location of the individual icons within the window. Make sure the window to Snapshot is active. Most of the icons are usually correct and only one may need moving to a better position. The fewer the icons you select and move into position, the quicker Snapshot executes.

- Open the Workbench diskette window by double clicking on it.

- Use the sizing gadget to enlarge the size of the Workbench diskette window as much as possible.

- Move one of the icons to a new location in the Workbench diskette window.

- Select the submenu item Contents from the Snapshot item of the **Windows** menu.

- Close the Workbench diskette window by double clicking on it.

- Open the Workbench diskette window by double clicking on its icon.

Note that the location of the icons within the window has been updated. A Snapshot of their location has been stored on your diskette.

Show

This item contains two submenu items, Only Icons and All Files. This is a new and powerful addition to Workbench 2.0. Workbench 1.3 could only show icons in windows. Workbench 2.0 allows you to show Only Icons or All Files in your windows.

- Open the RAM Disk by double clicking on its icon.

The RAM disk contains no icons, yet 7K is in use. What is occupying these 7K of memory?

- Select the All Files submenu item from the Show item in the **Windows** menu.

The RAM disk now contains icons for env, t and clipboard drawers. The env drawer contains important information about the Amiga's operating system environment. The t drawer is used to store temporary files. The clipboard drawer is the temporary storage area for text and drawings that are place in the clipboard. These drawers are used by the operating system and are usually not accessed by the average Amiga user. The Amiga's operating system knows this and therefore does not clutter up the display by showing these files.

View by   This item contains four submenu items, Icon, Name, Date and Size. This is a new and powerful addition to Workbench 2.0. Workbench 1.3 could only show icons in windows. Workbench 2.0 allows you to show icons as well as filenames in your windows.

- Open the Workbench diskette window by double clicking on it.

- Enlarge the size of the Workbench diskette window as much as possible using the sizing gadget.

- Select the Name submenu item from the View by item in the **Windows** menu.

The display changes and the files are displayed by name. Additional information is displayed concerning the size or type of file, the file attributes and the creation date of the file. Experiment selecting various options of the View by menu item. Select the All Files submenu item from the Show item and notice how disordered the display becomes when all the files are displayed by name.

The various file display methods can be quite useful since files may be displayed by name, date and size. The ability to display all files on the Workbench screen is also a new addition to Workbench 2.0. Workbench 1.3 could only display all the files on a diskette from the CLI.

The icon display will be the one you use most with your Amiga, so when you are finished experimenting with the various displays return to the normal icon display.

- Select the Only Icons submenu item from the Show item in the **Windows** menu.

- Select the Icon submenu item from the View by item in the **Windows** menu.

Icons

The **Icons** menu contains all functions relating to icons. You must select an icon on the screen before using an item in the **Icons** menu.

Open   Opens the selected icons. This is the same as using the mouse to double click on the icon.

- Select the icon you want to open.

- Choose Open from the **Icons** menu.

Copy   Select this item to copy disks, icons, files, drawers and entire diskettes.

You'll use this item in backing up your important diskettes. Note that you can only make a copy of a disk onto another disk.

The disk you want to copy is called the source disk or the FROM disk. Before using the Copy item, make sure to write protect the source disk. The disk which you are copying to is called the destination disk or TO.

- Insert the source disk into the internal drive (DF0:).

- Select the icon corresponding to the source disk.

- Choose Copy from the **Icons** menu

Follow the prompts on the screen.

Rename   You may want to rename icons to better clarify their contents.

- Select the icon which you want to rename.

- Choose rename from the **Icons** menu.

A requester will appear prompting you to enter the new name.

- Use the Del key to erase the old name. You can also press the right <Amiga> key and X to erase the entire text gadget.

- Enter the new name for the icon. Do not include spaces before or following the new name.

- Press the ⇧ key to close the requester.

Information
Displays important information about selected icons. This information includes the icon name, size, stack (memory available for a specific tool), the current status of the icon and other diskette information.

- Select the icon.

- Choose information from the Icons menu.

Save any changes in this window by selecting the Save gadget or select Cancel to close the window without saving any changes.

Snapshot   Use Snapshot to save the location of individually selected icons. This is useful if you want, for example, to keep the Workbench icon in the upper left of the screen.

- Select the icon(s) which you would like to snapshot.

- Choose `Snapshot` from the **Icons** menu.

The next time you open the window the icons will appear in the same position.

Note that using the `Clean Up` item may change the current positions of the icons.

UnSnapshot

Removes the snapshot information from the icons in the active window.

- Select the icon(s) which you would like to use to delete the snapshot.

- Choose `UnSnapshot` from the **Icons** menu.

The next time you open the window, Workbench automatically places the icon(s) at any location on the screen.

Leave Out   You may want to remove an icon from a window and place it into the Workbench window. This icon may be one you often use but you have to open a disk and several drawers to open it.

To access this icon faster, use `Leave Out` to move the icon to the Workbench disk.

- Select the icon which you want to move.

- Choose the `Leave Out` from the **Icons** menu.

The exception to the `Leave Out` item is the `Trashcan`. It must remain in the Workbench.

Put Away   You can use `Put Away` to return the icon moved in Leave Out to its original drawer.

- Select the icon in the Workbench window to `Put Away`.

- Choose `Put Away` from the **Icons** menu.

Delete   As you continue to use your Amiga, the number of files and icons may increase to the point that there is no room for additional data on the disk. Therefore you may need to delete some of the files and their icons.

Be careful with `Delete`. Once an icon is deleted, you cannot access its information.

- Select the icon you want to delete.

Remember, you can use the drag selection or extended selection if you're deleting more than one icon.

- Choose `Delete` from the **Icons** menu.

A requester appears on the screen to confirm that you want to delete the files and drawers. If you're unsure at this point, select the CANCEL gadget.

- Select the OK gadget to delete the selected file(s) and drawer(s).

Format Disk

You must format a new diskette or a non-AmigaDOS diskette before you can use it to store data. We discussed how and why you need to format a diskette in Section 2.5.

Before formatting the diskette, remember that formatting it erases all information from the diskette.

- Insert the disk you want to format into any disk drive. Select its corresponding disk icon. This appears as DF0:???? or DF1:???? or other depending on the disk drive.

- Then choose `Format` from the **Icons** menu.

Two additional notes on using `Format`...:

1. You do not have to use `Format` if the unformatted disk is the destination disk during a `Copy` item. The destination disk is automatically formatted during a `Copy`.

2. Another screen appears if you are formatting a new blank disk. The Amiga cannot recognize the unformatted diskette. Select the Continue gadget to continue with the format.

Empty Trash

Deletes the unneeded files in the `Trashcan`. You must select the `Trashcan` in order to empty its contents.

- Drag the icon over the `Trashcan`.

- Select the `Trashcan` (the lid will open) and choose `Empty Trash` from the **Icons** menu.

Tools

Contains additional tools accessible from the Workbench.

ResetWB

Resets the Workbench.

Workbench 1.3 menus

This section will present the individual menus of Workbench 1.3 in the order in which they appear on the screen.

Workbench	Disk	Special
Open	Empty Trash	Clean up
Close	Initialize	Last Error
Duplicate		Redraw
Rename		Snapshot
Info		Version
Discard		

Workbench

Open   Opens the selected icons. This is the same as double clicking on the icon.

Close   Closes selected windows. These windows can correspond to drawers or entire diskettes.

Duplicate   Copies selected icons, these can be files, drawers and entire diskettes.

Rename   Renames selected icons.

Info   Displays important information about selected icons.

Discard   Deletes selected icons.

Disk

Empty Trash
Deletes the files in the Trashcan. The Trashcan must be selected in order to empty it.

Initialize
Formats the selected diskette, all information is erased from the diskette.

Special

The **Special** menu has five items. Most of these items are ghost items right now.

Clean Up   This item puts icons in a selected drawer or diskette into neat order.

- Double-click the Workbench diskette icon.

- Double-click the System drawer to open it.

- Drag a few icons to different places in the **System** window.

- Click once on the System drawer icon to activate it.

- Select the **Special** pulldown menu.

- Select the Clean Up item, and watch the **System** window.

The Amiga automatically tidies up the **System** window. You can also clean up entire diskettes:

- Double-click the Workbench diskette icon.

- Drag a few icons to different places in the **Workbench** window.

- Click once on the Workbench diskette icon to activate it.

- Select the **Special** pulldown menu.

- Select the Clean Up item, and watch the **Workbench** window.

Remember that Clean Up works only on active diskettes or drawer icons.

- Open the Utilities drawer.

- Drag the icons to different places in the **Utilities** window.

- Select Clean Up from the **Special** pulldown menu.

Nothing happens, because the Utilities drawer needs activation. An active window is not enough.

- Click on the Utilities drawer to activate it.

- Select Clean Up from the **Special** pulldown menu.

Last Error

This item redisplays the last error detected by the Amiga. There is no error when this item appears in ghost print.

The following is an intentional error to demonstrate this item:

- Drag the Workbench diskette icon up to the top of the Workbench screen.

Notice the screen flashes and the Workbench diskette icon reappears at its previous location. The title bar displays the Icons cannot be moved into this window error message.

- Click somewhere on the Workbench screen.

The message disappears. Suppose you didn't see that error message, and wanted to know what it said:

- Select Last Error from the **Special** pulldown menu.

The error message reappears on the title bar. It will reappear each time you select Last Error. The message changes when another error occurs.

Other common error messages include:

disk write-protected

disk full

object not found

Redraw Sometimes programs will disrupt a part of the screen. When this occurs select **Redraw** from the **Special** pulldown menu. This item restores the open windows to their original appearance. This is one of the few Amiga items which you can access any time.

- Open a few diskette icons and drawer icons. Next select **Redraw** from the **Special** menu.

The windows on the Workbench flash and their displays are updated from memory.

Snapshot The Snapshot item takes a "screen photo."

- If the Utilities drawer is still open from above, close it.

- Double-click the Utilities drawer icon.

Extended selection lets you activate several icons at the same time. Simply press one of the ⇧ keys and click once on every icon you want selected.

- Press and hold a ⇧ key.

- Select all the icons inside the **Utilities** window.

- Select the Snapshot item from the **Special** pulldown menu.

The disk drive runs, and nothing appears to happen.

- Close the **Utilities** window, and reopen the Utilities drawer.

Snapshot allows you to determine the positions of the individual icons within a window, the window size and the point on the screen at which it appears.

- Use the sizing gadget to reduce the size of the **Utilities** window as much as possible.

- Drag the **Utilities** window to the lower right corner of the Workbench screen.

- Click once on the Utilities drawer icon in the **Workbench** window.

- Select Snapshot from the **Special** pulldown menu.

- Close and reopen the **Utilities** window.

Snapshot ensures that the window reopens at the size and location at which you set the window when you selected Snapshot. It's unnecessary to select all the icons. Most of them are usually correct, and only one may need moving to a better position. The fewer the icons you select and move into position, the quicker Snapshot executes.

Version

This item is of interest only if you want to know the version number of your Workbench diskette.

- Select the Version item from the **Special** pulldown menu.

Version numbers of the Workbench change as the developers of the Amiga improve the Workbench programming. As long as your version number is higher than 33.56, there should be no problem.

2.13   Amiga additions

In this section we'll discuss the several hardware changes which you can eventually make to your Amiga configuration. There are a number of pieces of hardware currently available for improving your Amiga.

Check with your dealer to get an idea of the current capabilities of your Amiga. You may be surprised by the possibilities offered by your Amiga.

Modulator

A modulator allows you to connect your Amiga to a color television through the RGB output jack behind the Amiga. One end of the cable plugs into the modulator and the other end connects to the television's antenna input.

The modulator has three connections:

1. **RF-Out** sends the combined audio and video signals to the television.

2. **Video Out** connects the modulator to a color video recorder. This lets you record special effects and animation onto videotape from your Amiga.

3. **Audio In** transmits the Amiga's sound system to the television, monitor or video recorder. You remember working with the Y cable in Chapter 1. Instead of plugging the single end of the Y cable into a monitor, you plug it into the **Audio In** jack.

Memory expansion

If you own an Amiga 500 which has not been expanded, one alert or error message, which you may see frequently, is Not Enough Memory. This occurs at different times on a 512K Amiga. The original Amiga 1000 came with 256K, so this error occurred more often on the 1000 models.

Most Amiga programs now on the market require at least 512K so memory expansion is a necessity if you own an Amiga 1000.

For Amiga 500 users, there's another advantage to purchasing more memory. The memory expansion currently available for the Amiga 500 allows more use of the RAM disk, and a permanent clock. Since this expansion is battery-powered, the clock stays on constantly.

Memory expansion can be added by your local dealer. The expansion board plugs into the housing underneath the Amiga 500, and the Amiga 2000 and 3000 accepts an expansion board on the expansion bus of the central processing unit.

NOTE: Some early software may not run with the added memory on the Amiga 500. If this happens, use the NoFastMem program from the System drawer before running the problem program. This program disables the memory expansion in the Amiga 500.

Disk drives An external disk drive makes copying, initializing and program and file storage much easier. See the section on "Interfaces and expansion" for information on connecting an external disk drive.

MIDI Interface A MIDI interface allows the Amiga to control professional music synthesizers. MIDI stands for Musical Instrument Digital Interface.

Genlock Genlocks are devices that synchronize your computer's video output and an external video source, such as a video camera or VCR. With a VCR and a genlock on your Amiga you could have your own mini-video studio.

Digitizers A digitizer allows you to capture color screen pictures. The Amiga's high resolution modes allow almost photographic quality images to be loaded, edited and stored in your computer.

3
AmigaBASIC

3.   AmigaBASIC

AmigaBASIC is the Amiga's implementation of the *BASIC* language. BASIC is an acronym for Beginner's All-purpose Symbolic Instruction Code. It's only one of the many computer languages available. Although AmigaBASIC is much slower than other languages, such as *C*, a new user can easily learn how to use it.

This chapter prepares you for your first contact with the AmigaBASIC language. However, don't expect a complete tutorial of BASIC. There isn't enough room in this book to include a complete guide to BASIC for the beginner. Just consider the fact that *AmigaBASIC Inside and Out* from Abacus contains over 500 pages. If you need a BASIC book which will teach you the language to advanced levels, *AmigaBASIC Inside and Out* is the book for you.

This chapter covers three major subjects. The first section introduces the AmigaBASIC demo programs on the AmigaBASIC diskette. These will give you an idea of what AmigaBASIC will do for you. These demos, written by Commodore development personnel, demonstrate the Amiga's extensive capabilities.

The next section describes writing programs in AmigaBASIC. Even the simplest listing becomes impossible if you don't know where and how to enter it. This applies especially to the Amiga because it's very different from BASIC versions which other computers use. This second part gives you enough background to enter AmigaBASIC listings from computer magazines or books.

The remaining sections of this chapter contain short and easily entered programs involving graphics, sound and animation. These programs give you a chance to understand the program structure in your AmigaBASIC manual. We recommend that you study that manual and its sample programs before you try the programs in Section 3.5 through Section 3.10. Figure out the major program logic on your own using this chapter, the AmigaBASIC manual and the short explanations in the listings.

If you discover that you won't get much further in BASIC without help, many books on the subject of AmigaBASIC can help.

The main thing to keep in mind during this chapter is: Programming is the only way to learn programming.

3.1 The Extras diskette

The diskette named Amiga Extras 1.3 contains more than just AmigaBASIC.

If you're using Workbench 2.0, the AmigaBASIC diskette is available from your local dealer. Contact your dealer or Commodore for more information.

- Insert the Extras diskette into the drive.

As usual, a diskette icon appears on the **Workbench** window. It has the name Extras.

- Double-click the Extras diskette icon.

Don't worry if the contents in your Extras disk are different. The contents of this diskette occasionally change so it's hard to say exactly what your particular copy of the Extras diskette will contain. However, we're only concerned right now with two icons on this disk. AmigaBASIC and BasicDemos. The drawer labeled FD1.3 is also extremely important. None of these files are of direct use to you, but the programs contained in the BasicDemos drawer won't function without them. Never experiment with the FD1.3 drawer.

Usually the rest of these icons become interesting once you have experience in programming AmigaBASIC.

- **If you haven't already done so, please make a backup copy of the Extras diskette.**

See the section on the System drawer in Chapter 2 for information on Diskcopy. This chapter assumes that you have a copy of the Extras diskette.

This window contains several icons. There is a Trashcan icon, which appears on all Amiga diskettes. There are also two drawer icons. One has the name BasicDemos and the other has the name Tools.

• Double-click the BasicDemos icon.

Your disk drive runs, and a window named BasicDemos appears.

• Enlarge the BasicDemos window so that you can see everything on it.

BASIC icons

A number of icons, which look like dog-eared pages, appear on the screen. Some of these icons look like typed pages, while others have drawings on them. The typed pages are data files generated by and read from a program. Some of these are function libraries that allow AmigaBASIC to do even more than it already can. As a beginner you really don't need to know much more about them. See your Amiga's BASIC manual for more information.

• Double-click the Music icon in the BasicDemos window.

If your Amiga is near your stereo system, you can connect the Amiga sound outputs to the auxiliary inputs of the stereo. To write something like this you almost have to know more about music than programming. However, the most important thing about this program is that it is written in BASIC.

• Close the Music window by clicking on its close gadget.

The functions of the other demos you'll find here become more interesting once you get more involved in AmigaBASIC. If you'd like to know what each program does, load the file named List-ME. It gives you details about the programs not described here. All of the demos start with a double-click, just like any other Amiga program.

Screen

This is a good demonstration of the Amiga's object graphics and color. The sizes of the squares change in proportion if you change the window's size. The Amiga selects colors at random.

NOTE:

It's possible that a demo program will stop at a certain point. Then the Amiga beeps, and a requester saying Illegal function call or a similar error message appears. A window labeled LIST appears, and another window may appear as well.

• Click the OK gadget in the requester.

• Click on the close gadgets of the two windows as soon as they become visible.

127

The normal Workbench screen reappears, and you can restart the same program or start another program.

ObjEdit

ObjEdit is the abbreviation for *Object Editor*. You'll use this program to create *bobs* and *sprites* on the Amiga. Bobs and sprites are graphic shapes that you can move across the screen quite easily using BASIC commands without disturbing the background.

NOTE:

When you work with ObjEdit, be sure to save your work at regular intervals.

Library

This program shows that an AmigaBASIC program can call different fonts, font sizes and type styles. However, this requires a certain amount of programming knowledge, as with most of these demo programs. Clicking on the close gadget ends the program.

Speech

The Amiga can also speak. The BASICDemos window has a demo program for this as well.

• Double-click the Speech icon in the BASICDemos window.

The Amiga says, Please--type what you want me to say. A string gadget appears, into which you type a sentence.

• Type in any sentence and press the ⏎ key at the end of your entry.

The voice quality changes when you adjust the sliders underneath the string gadget. These parameters are for voice quality:

Pitch	The voice's pitch (frequency).
Inflection	Type of vocal inflection.
Rate	Rate of speed for speech.
Voice	Voice gender.
Tune	Sets changes in voice quality.
Volume	Loudness.

The best way to find out how to use these controls is to actually use them.

• Type in the sentence I'M WORKING WITH WINDOWS and press the ⏎ key at the end of your entry.

Now let's go through the controls one by one.

• Click on the right of the Pitch slider, or drag it all the way to the right.

• Press the ⏎ key.

The Amiga voice now sounds high.

• Set Pitch to the level you like best.

• Click on the right of the Inflection slider, or drag it all the way to the right.

• Press the ⏎ key.

This moves all the way to the right or all the way to the left only. The right hand setting makes the Amiga speak with no inflection.

• Click on the right of the Rate slider, or drag it all the way to the right.

• Press the ⏎ key.

• Once you've heard how fast the Amiga can say things, set the slider to a speed you can understand.

• Click on the right of the Voice slider, or drag it all the way to the right.

• Press the ⏎ key.

This slider can be all the way left or all the way right only. It controls the gender of the voice (male or female).

• Click on the left of the Tune slider, or drag it all the way to the left.

• Press the ⏎ key.

The Tune slider alters the pronunciation speed of individual letters.

The last slider, the Volume slider, turns the volume up or down. Remember that its maximum is only as loud as the monitor's volume setting.

Each parameter which you set with the sliders can be operated with BASIC commands (more about this later).

• Click on the close gadget to close Speech.

• Double-click on the Picture icon.

Although an oval appears in the upper left corner of the screen, nothing else seems to happen.

• Move the pointer onto the screen and press the left mouse button.

The upper left corner of the picture appears at the pointer's current location. Keeping the left mouse button pressed lets you drag the picture around.

The programs behind these demos are often not so difficult to write as they might seem. This chapter is here to help you in the first steps of BASIC programming.

• Click on the Picture window's close gadget.

• Close the BASICDemos window.

Demo

This program demonstrates some neat color graphics and multitasking. The Amiga opens four windows each drawing separate graphics.

Don't worry if your Extras diskette does not contain all of the programs mentioned. The Extras diskette is extra and does change. See the README and LIST-ME files on the diskette for more information.

If your dealer or local user group has a copy of Workbench 1.2 get a copy of it and try the following demo. The Heart.ILBM file was removed from Workbench 1.3 because of space limitations.

• Double-click the LoadILBM-SaveACBM icon in the BasicDemos window.

Interchange
File Format

Most of the directions are on the screen already. You may wonder what ILBM files are. All you really need to know for now is that a few inventive programmers created a standard format for saving and loading data. This format, known also as the *Interchange File Format (IFF)*, is often a critical factor in drawing and painting programs, since it allows you to interchange drawings between programs. It's even possible to use IFF pictures in animation programs. This makes you, the consumer, independent of individual manufacturers. If you like manufacturer X's drawing program, but prefer manufacturer Y's animation program, they will still be just as compatible as if you had bought both programs from the same company. Just be sure the programs use IFF format.

Also, you can use the IFF pictures created by these programs in your own BASIC programs. As we mentioned, it's possible to write a game which uses pictures made with another graphic program. You can do this by using one of the programs on the Extras diskette designed for transferring graphics from one program to another.

• Enter Heart.ILBM and press the ⏎ key at the ILBM filespec? prompt.

• Press the ⏎ key at the ACBM-filespec? prompt.

The disk drive runs, and loads pictures of the Jarvik-7 artificial heart and a natural heart. A simple drawing program created this picture. This gives you an idea of what you can achieve after you've worked with your Amiga for a while.

NOTE:

The movement in the `Heart.ILBM` file is *cycle animation*, not true animation. Almost every Amiga drawing program in existence has this feature.

The program shows the picture for only 20 seconds. To change this, you'd have to change the program itself. As a beginner you're probably not familiar enough yet with your Amiga to change that program. Besides, this is one of the more complicated programs on the diskette.

3.2   Starting AmigaBASIC

Now that you have seen more or less of everything in the Extras window, it's time to start AmigaBASIC.

- Double-click the AmigaBASIC icon.

You'll hear the disk drive run as your Amiga loads AmigaBASIC in memory.

In a moment two windows appear on the screen: The LIST window and the BASIC window.

- Click once on the BASIC window.

In principle these windows work just like the Workbench window. Move the pointer anywhere in the BASIC window and click once. If you did this right, the Amiga confirms it by displaying OK.

The Workbench is in the background. If you want to see it, you only have to close the LIST window and the BASIC window. For now, however, keep the BASIC and LIST windows open.

3.3   First steps in BASIC

In this section we'll discuss the principles of BASIC programming. We'll start with a few basic rules and move up to the first program. Each command will appear in the left margin of the page and is followed by a description.

Although we'll list each command in uppercase letters, you do not have to use uppercase letters when writing programs.

COMMAND

For example, this is the format for a command and its description. The program lines you should enter will appear indented and in a typewriter-style font (Courier):

```
PRINT "This is a sample program line."
```

The BASIC window has several functions. First, it displays everything which a program produces as output.

*   Close the LIST window.

This automatically opens the BASIC window. Note the information in the upper left corner of the BASIC window. It displays the BASIC name (Commodore AmigaBASIC), its version number, when it was made, the developer (Microsoft Corp.), and the number of *bytes* free in both the system and in BASIC (see Appendix B for a definition of bytes).

Type the following:

*   CLS ⏎

Pressing the ⏎ key after a command *executes*, or performs, that command.

CLS

CLS (CLear Screen) clears all text and graphics from the BASIC window. Perhaps you're wondering why you need to press the ⏎ key. AmigaBASIC is an *interpreted* language. The AmigaBASIC interpreter translates your commands into a form the Amiga understands. Pressing ⏎ sends the command to the interpreter.

The language the Amiga understands consists of only two numbers: 0 and 1. Computers understand two conditions; power on and power off. Each time you input CLS, the interpreter translates it into a set of *binary numbers* (numbers in base 2), which looks something like 00000111010011001010011010101.

Type the following:

* `My name is Napoleon.`

In order for your Amiga to accept this statement, you must tell the BASIC interpreter to translate it:

* Press the ⊖ key.

The Amiga beeps once, changes the screen color and displays an *error requester* which says something similar to `Undefined Subprogram` at the top of the screen.

* Click on the `OK` gadget in the error requester.

When you press ⊖, the BASIC interpreter looks to see whether or not `My name is Napoleon` is a BASIC command. Since there is no such command, the Amiga gives an error message. This error message also informs you why it can't execute this line. This error requester disappears when you click on the `OK` gadget.

When you entered the sentence above, you noticed the small orange box which moved along as you typed. This is the *BASIC cursor*. It shows your position on the screen.

PRINT

`PRINT` performs output in the `BASIC` window. You may wonder why its known as PRINT when your Amiga isn't using a printer. The word comes from the early days of computing when output went directly to a printer instead of a screen.

* Type the following line:

`PRINT Christian Spanik` ⊖

The Amiga will display two zeros. The Amiga assumed here that `Christian Spanik` was a pair of *variables*. Variables are letters or even combinations of letters which are assigned certain values. Since neither `Christian` nor `Spanik` contains a number, the Amiga returned two zeros.

If you want the Amiga to display exactly what you enter, then you must enclose the words in quotation marks. Any text you place between quotation marks appears on the screen. The quotation marks do not appear on the screen.

* Type the line:

`PRINT "Christian Spanik"` ⊖

The words `Christian Spanik` appear in the `BASIC` window.

You can type your own name if you prefer.

You can also calculate with PRINT:

- Type the following line:

    PRINT 10/2 ⏎

Note that we did not use quotation marks in this command line. The Workbench Calculator showed you that the standard character for computer division is the slash (/), instead of the normal division sign (÷). The Amiga displays the result of 10/2 on the screen.

NOTE:
There is a difference between 0 (zero) and O (the letter O) inside the computer. Make sure that you always type ⓪ for zero and Ⓞ for the letter.

The result of our calculation is 5. If you wanted 10/2 and not 5 displayed, the line would read PRINT "10/2" ⏎. The output reproduces the figures entered between the quotation marks. Now combine both types of output:

- Type in the following line:

    PRINT "10/2="10/2 ⏎

? is the abbreviation for PRINT.

- Type in the following line:

    ?"10 divided by 2 is"10/2 ⏎

Direct mode
Entering commands which the computer immediately executes is called *direct mode*. You can do much more than that in direct mode, however.

X and Y are universal variables in math. They'll appear wherever two variables are required in a calculation.

- Type in the following line:

    ?X/Y ⏎

The Amiga beeps once, changes the screen color and displays an *error requester* which says Division by Zero.

Neither you nor your Amiga can divide numbers by zero. The computer read the above line as: Divide X by Y.

- Click on the OK gadget in the error requester.

The Amiga responds with OK.

Scrolling

Don't worry if you're running out of space at the bottom of the window. AmigaBASIC allows you to *scroll*. When there is no more room at the bottom, the Amiga allows one of the lines at the top to disappear and uses the space now available at the bottom. This is called scrolling. In direct mode, the line rolls up out of the top of the screen.

Similar to the example above (PRINT Christian Spanik), the Amiga views X and Y as variables. Try division with combinations of letters:

    ?Christian/Spanik ⏎

The Amiga again displays an error requester which informs you that you attempted a division by zero.

AmigaBASIC assigns each variable which doesn't have a value of 0. This means that BASIC reads ?X/Y as "Print 0/0." Christian and Spanik were read as variables above and AmigaBASIC assigned them zeros. If you want to check the value of each variable:

    ?X:?Y:?Christian Spanik

LET

All four variables come up 0. You can change this by assigning values to variables. There are two ways to assign values to variables. The most common method is to use LET.

    LET y=5 ⏎

Make sure that there is a space between the LET and the y. The Amiga responds with OK. When an OK appears, this means that AmigaBASIC accepted this entry.

• Type in the following line:

    ?x/y ⏎

This time the result is 0.

• Type in the following line:

    LET y=2 ⏎
    LET x=10 ⏎
    ?x/y ⏎

You can calculate using these placeholders.

• Type in the following line:

    let christian=100 ⏎
    let chris=50 ⏎
    ?(x/y)+(christian-chris)*y*x ⏎

The parentheses force the Amiga to process the individual math functions in the right order. The result is 1005.

By now it should be clear that the direct mode also has its disadvantages. It's very good for short statements, but it just doesn't work when more complex things are involved. Also, you can't make corrections in direct mode; incorrect lines have to be retyped. Finally, a line is gone when it scrolls up past the top of the BASIC window.

Program mode

The LIST window allows you to operate in *program mode*. That is, you can enter programs in the LIST window, correct them, look through the entire program and scroll through program code.

•   Press and hold the right mouse button.

A pulldown menu bar appears at the top. This menu bar has four titles:

        Project   Edit   Run   Windows

•   Select the Show List item from the **Windows** pulldown menu.

The LIST window reappears. The BASIC cursor appears in the LIST window.

•   Type in the following:

        ?"Hello" ⏎

The text doesn't appear in the BASIC window but ? changes into the word PRINT. The BASIC cursor moves down one line but there is still no output.

•   Type in the following:

        print "Hello"

•   Don't press the ⏎ key yet.

The word print remains in lower case.

•   Press the ⬆ (Cursor up) key.

The only change is that print becomes PRINT. The program still has yet to run.

Program mode is the mode in which you write a program. The lines above are a simple program.

You may have already looked at some books on BASIC programming. Most versions of BASIC use line numbers to help the computer process commands in order. AmigaBASIC doesn't use line numbers.

The Amiga doesn't need or use line numbers because it uses a separate window for entering programs. This window is called the LIST window. A normal BASIC listing could look like this:

```
10 PRINT "Hello"
20 PRINT "Hello"
```

Simply by looking at this listing, you should see that this program prints Hello on the screen twice.

The BASIC window is also called the *output window*. This is a window used for output (display).

You now, therefore, have one window for output and one window for entering the program lines.

• Activate the BASIC window.

When the BASIC cursor reappears, you can again make direct mode input.

• Type in the following line in the BASIC window:

    RUN ⏎

The LIST window disappears and the word Hello appears twice on the BASIC window.

• Type in the following line in the BASIC window:

    RUN ⏎

The screen clears and the word Hello appears twice on the BASIC window.

RUN

The Amiga must use a command to execute a BASIC program. This command is called RUN. You can now enter RUN as often as you like. The Amiga processes your program whenever you enter this command.

In summary, write programs in the LIST window. This is where the Amiga automatically notes the commands and their sequence. You then execute commands directly by writing them in the BASIC window.

The LIST window closes when your program executes.

• Press and hold the right mouse button.

• Select Show List from the **Window** pulldown menu.

The LIST window appears on the screen.

• Press and hold the right mouse button.

- Move the pointer to the **Window** pulldown menu.

Keyboard shortcuts

Note that an **A** and an L appear to the right of the Show List menu item. You remember keyboard shortcuts from your work with the Notepad in Chapter 2. **A** represents the right <Amiga> key; the L is quite simply the L key.

- Type RUN or run in the BASIC window and press the ⏎ key.

You can use uppercase or lowercase letters, or both in combination. As soon as the program runs, the LIST window disappears. Now you can try the keyboard shortcut.

- Press and hold the right <Amiga> key and press the L key.

The program listing reappears. Sometimes it's easier and more practical using keyboard shortcuts than using the mouse.

The LIST window and the BASIC window now stand next to each other on the screen. Let's look more closely at this first BASIC program.

There is nothing in the LIST window but PRINT "Hello" twice. Just Hello appears twice in the BASIC window. The listing appears in the LIST window, while the BASIC window shows the results of the program.

- Press and hold the right mouse button.

- Select Show List from the **Window** pulldown menu.

- Activate the LIST window by moving the mouse pointer into the LIST window and pressing the mouse button.

Your BASIC cursor should now be somewhere within the LIST window. It's not easy to see at first.

Cursor keys and editing

Working on an AmigaBASIC program consists of two parts: writing the program and then correcting any programming errors. This paragraph is about the correction phase, or *editing*.

The ⏎ key is important when programming in most versions of BASIC. This key ends a line of input and sends the line to the interpreter. In the LIST window of AmigaBASIC, all you need to press is a cursor key when editing to accept an edited line.

There are, however, a few exceptions to this rule. We've previously discussed one of the primary functions of the editor: moving the BASIC cursor by using the cursor keys.

- Activate the LIST window.

- Press and hold the ⊡ (Cursor down) key.

In a moment the Amiga beeps and the screen changes color. The reason for this is that you cannot move the BASIC cursor past the end of a program with the cursor keys. You can do this only with the ⏎ key, since it extends to the end of the program.

The computer must know the length and ending point of the program. If you need additional space, you must tell your Amiga to form a new line (by pressing the ⏎ key). This saves space when later saving the program to diskette.

- Position the BASIC cursor directly below the last line.

- Type in:

```
?"Hello" ⏎
```

The Amiga now displays ?"Hello" three times on the LIST window. Run this program again to check this out. This time, don't type RUN in the BASIC window. Instead, use the Start item from the **Run** pulldown menu:

- Press and hold the right mouse button.

- Select the Start item from the **Run** pulldown menu.

If your LIST window is active when you select Start, then the following happens: The Amiga displays Hello in the BASIC window three times, the program ends and the LIST window activates again. The listing disappeared as soon as the program executed. If the BASIC window is active, the LIST window disappears and remains hidden. If the LIST window is active, it reappears after the program executes. You'll see the advantages of this in the course of the next few pages.

The Start item of the **Run** pulldown menu also has a keyboard shortcut: right <Amiga> Ⓡ.

Copying text

Let's suppose you want the program to display Hello 10 times in the BASIC window. You have two choices: You can type the same sentence seven more times or you can use the editor. The editor *copies* program text. Go to the **Edit** pulldown menu and select the Copy item. This item allows you to copy anything which is selected within the shaded area.

Until now, activating has meant clicking an icon. With Amiga's BASIC editor, this technique can mark and use certain parts of the screen, even for programming and editing programs.

- Move the mouse pointer to the left of the P in the first line.

- Press and hold the left mouse button.

• Drag the pointer past the last line.

Marking
blocks

Note that parts of the LIST window are now a different color. This color change is called *highlighting*, and this process is used in *marking blocks* for editing. You could have marked only one line or word as easily as you marked the entire program. If you make a mistake, click again somewhere to get rid of the highlighting. If you only want to mark a single word, double-click on that word. Try this with PRINT or Hello in your listing.

There is a second and somewhat more accurate method of marking whole blocks:

• Move the pointer to the required position and click once.

Make certain that the BASIC cursor which then appears is in the right place (before the first letter to appear inside the marking).

• Move the cursor to the position after the last letter to appear inside the marking.

• Press either one of the ⬆ keys and click the left mouse button.

• Mark the three PRINT "Hello" lines as a block.

• Select the Cut item from the **Edit** pulldown menu.

The three program lines disappear.

Cut

• Select the Paste item from the **Edit** pulldown menu.

Your program reappears. Now produce 10 program lines from these three.

Paste

• Mark the three PRINT "Hello" lines as a block.

• Select the Copy item from the **Edit** pulldown menu.

The Copy item only makes a copy of the marked program area. You need to tell your Amiga where to place the copied text.

Copy

• Position the cursor to the beginning of the line after the last program line.

• Select the Paste item from the **Edit** pulldown menu.

You now have six lines of PRINT "Hello".

• Select Paste again.

Now you have nine lines of PRINT "Hello" in your program.

- Select Paste again.

Now you have two lines too many; this was an intentional move.

- Mark the two extra PRINT lines as a block.

- Press the ⬅ (Backspace) key once.

Deleting text

Now you have ten PRINT commands after *deleting* the two extra program lines. Unlike Cut, which temporarily removes the marked block for pasting to a different section of the program, deleting permanently removes text. You cannot recover text removed by the ⬅ (Backspace) key.

Remember one thing when working with the **Edit** menu items: As soon as you put anything new in the memory used by Copy and Cut, any previous data is deleted. This means that the **Edit** items store a block only once.

FOR...NEXT

You may feel as if you've spent too much time on this program. There's an easier way to put the same message on the screen ten times. The solution is the FOR...NEXT *loop*. The word loop means that FOR...NEXT is placed around part of the program. Here's an easy way of writing a program which has the same result:

- Mark all the PRINT "Hello" lines except one as a block.

- Press the ⬅ (Backspace) key once.

- Position the BASIC cursor (with the cursor keys or the mouse) to the left of the PRINT of the remaining command and press the ⬅ key.

- Position the BASIC cursor to the top line (now blank) and type in:

    for x=1 to 10

- Position the BASIC cursor (with the cursor keys or the mouse) past the bottom line.

Note that the words for and to, written as lowercase letters, automatically change into uppercase letters. It prints all BASIC command words in uppercase. Letters or words which aren't BASIC commands remain as the programmer has entered them. This way you can quickly tell variables and placeholders from BASIC commands.

- Type in the following line:

    NEXT ⬅

The finished program should look like this:

```
For x=1 To 10
PRINT "Hello"
NEXT
```

• Run the program.

You'll get the same result but with a third of the programming effort and space as before.

END

END closes a program which works properly. If you do not use END to finish the program, the program does in fact stop, but for this demonstration an END is better.

• Be sure your LIST window is active.

• Position the BASIC cursor (with the cursor keys or the mouse) past the bottom line.

• Type in the following line:

    end ⏎

Your program should now look like this:

```
FOR x=1 TO 10
PRINT "Hello"
NEXT
END
```

• Select the Step item from the **Run** pulldown menu.

This clears the BASIC window. The only change to the LIST window is the frame surrounding the first program line.

• Select the Step item again (you can also press right <Amiga> T).

Now Hello appears in the BASIC window but only one time. Although nothing else happens, the program hasn't ended. An OK would appear below the Hello and the cursor would be visible if the program was executed.

But the LIST window changed as well. Now the second program line has a frame. And that line is the one with the PRINT "Hello". That is the command which the program executed, as you could see in the BASIC window.

Step lets you follow the program sequence line by line, as quickly or as slowly as you like. Selecting Step carries out the next command. If you want to run the whole program a little faster press the right <Amiga> T key combination as mentioned above.

The frame moves to the third line (NEXT). The more often you press it, the better you can observe the program sequence.

• Press right <Amiga> ⬚ᵀ until the program ends.

You know the program ends when END is framed and when you see 10 Hellos in the BASIC window. Now use the command Step to see how the FOR...NEXT loop works.

• Select Step again.

The frame surrounds the first program line. This line is the first command, as well as the first program step.

• Activate the BASIC window and enter:

    ?x ⏎

The Amiga returns a value of 1. The variable x clearly contains 1 now. So that you do not have to restart the program after this interruption, do the following:

• Click on the LIST window.

• Select Step again.

The Amiga goes on working from the point where it stopped before. Select Step until the frame is around NEXT.

• Click in the BASIC window.

• Enter:

    ?x ⏎

The value returned for x is now 2. The program hasn't returned to the first program line yet. So the addition to x must be in the middle two lines.

The second line writes Hello on the screen. Otherwise there is nothing there that makes the value for x increase. This leaves only the third line. And this can't be right, since it only says NEXT. To confirm this, do the following:

• Click on the LIST window.

• Select Step again until the frame returns to NEXT.

• Enter in the BASIC window:

    ?x ⏎

You get the expected 3, before the third Hello appears on the screen. The variable previously determined in the FOR instruction always increases by one when the NEXT instruction occurs.

- In the active BASIC window enter:

  x=10 ⏎

- Reactivate the LIST window.

- Select Step three times.

The computer accepts your entry and assigns the variable x a value of 10 and stops further execution of the program. This is because the maximum value determined in the first line has been exceeded.

To summarize, everything in a FOR...NEXT loop repeats and executes until the loop surpasses the loop limit set. In this case, PRINT "Hello" repeats ten times because the loop only ends at the value 10. The variable could also have been a y, a, b or X. The Amiga considers X and x two different variable names.

- Click within the LIST window.

Program structuring

The BASIC cursor appears. The parts of the program belonging together should be set apart for better readability. This can be done by indenting lines.

- Move the BASIC cursor before the F in the first line. Press the Spacebar once.

The NEXT belongs with the FOR, so indent this line one space to the right as well.

- Position the cursor in front of the N in NEXT. Press the Spacebar once.

Now move the statement PRINT "Hello" to the right past the FOR and the NEXT.

- Position the cursor in front of the P in PRINT. Press the Spacebar once.

The END can stay at its current location. Now when you look at the program, you can see that it's much easier to read. You should be able to tell what a short program, such as our Hello program, will do by simply reading it.

However, the longer and more complicated the program, the better program structures can help you quickly understand the connection between individual program sections.

- Position the cursor in front of the P in PRINT.

- Press the ⏎ key.

The Amiga automatically inserts the correct number of blanks between the left edge and the PRINT.

- Move the cursor back to this blank line and enter:

    ? "I am the program" ⏎

If you indented this instruction two spaces, like the other PRINT instruction, then you understand the principle of structured programming.

- Start the program.

If you want, you can indent the Hello a little more in the third program line, so that it fits in better with the I am the program. Simply insert a few spaces between the opening quotation mark and the Hello.

3.4   Saving programs

It only takes a moment to lose an entire day's work. All it requires is someone tripping over the power cord. There are thousands of other dangers which can kill or ruin a program. Tired programmers, angry mothers, little sisters, dogs, cats and electrical storms can all cut the power on computers. Therefore, you should get into a habit when programming; save as often as possible.

Save and exit

The Amiga offers you simple and convenient options for saving programs. It also tries to ensure that you do not accidentally forget to save your program. For example:

• Select the Quit item from the **Project** pulldown menu.

A requester appears prompting you to confirm if you want to save the program in memory before quitting.

• Click on the Yes gadget.

This tells the Amiga that you want to save the program. A new requester appears. Since you have not saved the program yet, the string gadget under the heading Save Program As: remains empty. If you previously saved the program, this string gadget would list the same name that you last assigned the program.

• Click in the string gadget.

• Type the name BasicDemos/Hello.

• Press the ⏎ key or click on the OK gadget.

The program is saved in the drawer named BASICDemos. To call it from there, the Extras diskette must be in the disk drive. After the program is saved, the Workbench screen reappears.

• Open the BASICDemos drawer.

• Double-click the Hello icon.

The program immediately executes. As soon as it is finished, you'll see the normal BASIC window displayed in front of you.

The following is a list of the menu items from the **Project** pulldown menu:

New   This item deletes the program in memory so you can begin work on a new program. The Amiga displays a requester asking you to confirm if you want to save the program currently in memory.

Open   This item allows you to call programs into memory without running them.

Save   Save if the program was previous saved. The Amiga
You   can automatically stores the program under the same name.
always   However, the Amiga overwrites the old program.
access

Save As   Save As lets you resave an edited program under a new name. The original program remains undisturbed under the old name and can be called back into memory if needed.

Quit   A requester appears which tells you the program still in memory was not saved to diskette. If you left BASIC in spite of this, then you would lose this data. Therefore, AmigaBASIC gives you the option of saving the program before continuing, leaving BASIC without quitting or cancelling the Quit item.

3.5   Four BASIC programs

All statements that you'll encounter in the following listings are mentioned in your Amiga's BASIC manual. Each program starts with a description of the problem that the program is supposed to solve. This way you understand exactly what the program is trying to achieve, and you may also want to try to write your own program to solve the problem and test your skill. We'll list all the statements in this description required in the program to solve the problem. Don't judge the success of your own program by how closely it coincides with the book version, but rather by whether it provides the correct solution. If you don't want to solve the problem on your own, simply go on to the program listing. Explanations follow the listings to show the logic behind the program structure. Should you encounter any statements that you aren't familiar with, look them up in your BASIC manual. Sometimes the manual has sample programs to clarify a statement's use.

When you see the ⏎ symbol, remember this is the ENTER or RETURN key. It signifies when you should press the ⏎ key. Program lines which must be on one line in AmigaBASIC may appear on two lines in this book. This symbol will clarify when you should press the ⏎ key.

3.6   Graphic program

The first problem involves the correct use of AREA and AREAFILL statements. The three-dimensional image comes from the proper use of the available colors.

Problem: Use only the Amiga's standard colors to draw an image of a three-dimensional cube. The program requires the COLOR, AREA and AREAFILL statements.

```
Cube: ⏎
  COLOR 3,0  ⏎
   AREA (199,149)  :  AREA (399,149)  ⏎
   AREA (399,49)   :  AREA (199,49)   ⏎
   AREAFILL ⏎
  COLOR 2,0  ⏎
   AREA (199,49)   :  AREA (399,49)   ⏎
   AREA (449,39)   :  AREA (249,39)   ⏎
   AREAFILL ⏎
   AREA (199,149)  :  AREA (149,149)  ⏎
   AREA (199,139)  ⏎
   AREAFILL ⏎
  COLOR 1,0  ⏎
   AREA (399,49)   :  AREA (449,39)   ⏎
   AREA (449,139)  :  AREA (399,149)  ⏎
   AREAFILL ⏎
```

Solution: This version of the program draws the cube in the approximate center of the screen using the AREA statement. COLOR 3, 0 sets the drawing color to orange (3) and the background color to blue (0). We'll assume that you're using the Workbench default color settings.

Four AREA statements set the four corners of the front side of the cube. The following AREAFILL statement then draws this front side onto the screen.

The COLOR 2, 0 statement sets the drawing color to black (2) while the background color remains blue. The Amiga next draws the top of the cube. Again, the four corner points are placed to make the cube look three-dimensional. The second area drawn here is the shadow on the left side of the cube. This requires a three-sided area only, since part of the shadow is hidden behind the cube.

In the last section the COLOR 1, 0 statement returns the colors to their standard setting (white on a blue background). This portion is at the end of the program so that the text output appears in the standard color settings after the program runs. With four vertices the program defines the white side panel of the cube. Thus, the imaginary light source stands to the very right of the cube. Again, the four corners are offset, creating the illusion of perspective. You may want to experiment further with these statements before continuing to the next problem.

3.7   Animation program

The advantage of this program is that you just wrote half of it (the cube). Now you just have to add the new section to the end of the existing program. The most difficult thing to understand in this program is the calling and reading of the bobs (movable objects). The statements used to move the bob are quite simple, since they are variations of the OBJECT. statement. You just have to take the time to learn the individual versions of the OBJECT. statement family. You'll have already taken the first step toward writing the solution to the next problem.

Problem: Expand the above cube program to work with a bob called ball. Read this ball in three times, so that three balls jump out of the inside of the cube. In addition to the statements required to form the cube, use the following statements in this program: OPEN...FOR INPUT AS; OBJECT.SHAPE; CLOSE; OBJECT.X; OBJECT.Y; OBJECT.HIT; OBJECT.AY; OBJECT.AX; OBJECT.ON; OBJECT.START.

```
Cube: ↵
COLOR 3,0 ↵
  AREA (199,149) : AREA (399,149) ↵
  AREA (399,49) : AREA (199,49) ↵
AREAFILL ↵
COLOR 2,0 ↵
  AREA (199,49) : AREA (399,49) ↵
  AREA (449,39) : AREA (249,39) ↵
AREAFILL ↵
  AREA (199,149) : AREA (149,149) ↵
  AREA (199,139) ↵
AREAFILL ↵
COLOR 1,0 ↵
  AREA (399,49) : AREA (449,39) ↵
  AREA (449,139) : AREA (399,149) ↵
AREAFILL ↵
    ↵
Balls: ↵
OPEN "Extras 1.3:BASICdemos/ball" FOR INPUT
AS 1 ↵
  Ball$=INPUT$(LOF(1),1) ↵
  FOR x=1 TO 3 ↵
    OBJECT.SHAPE x,Ball$ ↵
  NEXT x ↵
  CLOSE 1 ↵
  FOR x=1 TO 3 ↵
    OBJECT.X x,299 ↵
```

```
OBJECT.Y x,41  ⏎
OBJECT.HIT x,0,0  ⏎
OBJECT.AY x,-2  ⏎
NEXT x  ⏎
     ⏎
OBJECT.AX 1,-2  ⏎
OBJECT.AX 3,2  ⏎
FOR x=1 TO 3  ⏎
OBJECT.ON x  ⏎
OBJECT.START x  ⏎
NEXT x  ⏎
     ⏎
FOR x=1 TO 1400 : NEXT x  ⏎
FOR x=1 TO 3 : OBJECT.AY x,2 : NEXT x  ⏎
FOR x=1 TO 7000 : NEXT x  ⏎
```

Solution: The program section `Balls:` contains the new program code. First the program reads the ball from the `BASICDemos` drawer located on the `Extras` diskette. If you change the `Extras` diskette icon's name, you must also change the name in this program from `Extras` to the new name as well.

The program opens the bob file `ball FOR INPUT` so that it is read into memory as data file number 1. This file's contents go into the variable `Ball$:`. `INPUT$(LOF(1),1)` handles the `INPUT$` of the file number one. The following FOR...NEXT loop assigns the contents of `Ball$` to `OBJECTS` one through three, using `OBJECT.SHAPE`. The file closes.

The next section's FOR...NEXT loop counts from one to three. Here the following values are assigned to the three objects:

1) Their X-position (`OBJECT.X x,299`) 299 for all three objects.

2) Their Y-position (`OBJECT.Y x,41`) 41 for all three objects.

3) `OBJECT.HIT x,0,0` ensures that no collision interrupts occur when the balls collide with each other.

4) Their acceleration. Each of the three bobs receives a vertical acceleration of -2 with the `OBJECT.AY` statement. This means that each ball starts to move toward the top of the screen, moving an additional two pixels faster each second.

The third program block assigns the first and third bobs horizontal movement. Bob number one moves up and to the left, 2 pixels faster per second (-2). Bob number three moves to the right at the same rate (+2). Bob number two moves from bottom to top, without horizontal movement.

Another FOR...NEXT loop from 1 to 3 occurs. The three bobs turn on simultaneously and become visible (OBJECT.ON), while OBJECT.START starts the bob movement.

Next is a wait loop: FOR x=1 TO 1400:NEXT x. This loop gives the bobs enough time to get out from behind the upper screen border.

Once the first delay loop ends, the vertical (Y-) movements of the bobs "reverse." They are all set to positive (+2). The result: The original movement goes the opposite direction. The balls run slower, until the direction of flight changes again.

Another delay loop appears: FOR x=1 TO 7000: NEXT x.

3.8   Speech program

The speech programming of the Amiga is built on one statement. It must include several numerical parameters. Therefore, the most important thing is discovering exactly which numerical values deliver a nearly human voice. Once you've mastered that, you'll be mostly dealing with having your Amiga speak.

Problem: Write a program to simulate a conversation between an Amiga and an another 68000-based computer. Make the other machine speak slower and in a monotone. The necessary statements for this program: DATA; READ; SAY; TRANSLATE$.

```
Preparations: ⏎
 FOR x=0 TO 8 ⏎
  READ Amiga%(x) ⏎
 NEXT x ⏎
 FOR x=0 TO 8 ⏎
  READ Other%(x) ⏎
 NEXT x ⏎
 ⏎
Dialog: ⏎
 FOR x=1 TO 5 ⏎
  READ Amigatext$(x) ⏎
  READ Othertext$(x) ⏎
  SAY TRANSLATE$(Amigatext$(x)),Amiga% ⏎
  SAY TRANSLATE$(Othertext$(x)),Other% ⏎
 NEXT x ⏎
 ⏎
Vocaldata: ⏎
 ⏎
REM Amiga voice ⏎
DATA 120, 0, 173, 0, 22338, 64, 8, 0, 0 ⏎
REM "other" voice ⏎
DATA 232, 1, 84, 0, 17301, 64, 9, 0, 0 ⏎
 ⏎
REM Text: ⏎
DATA "Hello, I'm your Amiga." ⏎
DATA "Hello, I am one of the other sixty-
eight thousand based computers. I can speak
too." ⏎
DATA "That's interesting. How do you feel?"
DATA "Speaking is very difficult." ⏎
DATA "Well, I don't think so. Besides, it's
very helpful to the user." ⏎
```

```
DATA "Wait a moment, I seem to be having
memory trouble." ⏎
DATA "You are? Multitasking speech
synthesis is no problem for me." ⏎
DATA "I don't know the word multitasking.
Please explain." ⏎
DATA "But what can your user do with you if
you don't do multitasking?" ⏎
DATA "Excuse me, I feel some cherry bombs
coming on." ⏎
```

Solution: The most important commands are the different voice values for the two computers.

Preparations: reads the voice values for the Amiga and other voices. The values of these voices may take some experimentation (see *AmigaBASIC Inside and Out*, Chapter 6).

The array called Amiga% contains the Amiga voice parameters. The % extension means that this array contains only integer values. The SAY command requires integer parameters.

READ and DATA read in the values; the Amiga values appear in the listing under REM Voice of Amiga.

The array called Other% contains the other computer's voice parameters. The other computer values appear in the listing under REM Voice of "other" computer.

The main section of the program carries the name Dialog:.

The FOR...NEXT loop gives the number of exchanges between the Amiga and the other computer. FOR x=1 to 5 means 5 statements from the Amiga and 5 from the other computer.

READ reads in the AmigaText$, then Othertext$.

TRANSLATE$ translates the text into phonemes. The array names after the comma give the voice array. SAY says the text. The program accesses the Workbench file translator.library before saying anything; be sure your Workbench diskette is accessible.

3.9   Sound program

This program is somewhat more difficult than the previous programs.
This is because of the mathematical problems surrounding waveforms,
as well as the use of a new programming technique—*event trapping*.
Although reading pulldown menus and the mouse are among the
Amiga's best features, they're not the easiest to program.

Problem:

Write a program which produces sine waves, square waves and white
noise. The notes must be accessible through a mouse in a type of scale.
Mouse buttons must be pressed, and the mouse must be movable from
top to bottom. The three waveforms should be accessible from
pulldown menus.

```
Preparations: ⏎
 DIM Square%(255), Noise%(255) ⏎
 ⏎
MENU 1,0,1,"Program" ⏎
MENU 1,1,1,"->End<-" ⏎
MENU 2,0,1,"Waveform" ⏎
MENU 2,1,2," Sine" ⏎
MENU 2,2,1," Square" ⏎
MENU 2,3,1," Noise" ⏎
MENU 3,0,0,"" ⏎
MENU 4,0,0,"" ⏎
 ⏎
FOR x=0 TO 255 ⏎
IF x<128 THEN Square%(x)=127 ELSE
Square%(x)=-128 ⏎
Noise%(x)=RND*255-128 ⏎
IF INT(x/4)=x/4 AND x<190 THEN LINE(200,x)-
(400,x) ⏎
NEXT x ⏎
WAVE 0,SIN : Wform=1 ⏎
ON MENU GOSUB Menucontrol ⏎
ON MOUSE GOSUB Mousecontrol ⏎
MOUSE ON ⏎
MENU ON ⏎
 ⏎
Mainprogram: ⏎
GOTO Mainprogram ⏎
 ⏎
Menucontrol: ⏎
 Men=MENU(0) ⏎
 Item=MENU(1) ⏎
  IF Men=1 AND Item=1 THEN CLS: END ⏎
```

```
        IF Men=2 THEN  ⏎
        MENU 2,Wform,1  ⏎
        Wform=Item  ⏎
        MENU 2,Wform,2  ⏎
         IF Item=1 THEN  ⏎
          WAVE 0,SIN  ⏎
         ELSEIF Item=2 THEN  ⏎
          WAVE 0,Square%  ⏎
         ELSEIF Item=3 THEN  ⏎
          WAVE 0,Noise%  ⏎
         END IF  ⏎
        END IF  ⏎
        RETURN  ⏎
         ⏎
     Mousecontrol:  ⏎
      Mousevalue=MOUSE(0)  ⏎
      WHILE Mousevalue<0  ⏎
       Mousevalue=MOUSE(0)  ⏎
       SOUND 1200-(4.85*MOUSE(2)),1,127,0  ⏎
       FOR d=1 TO 90 : NEXT d  ⏎
      WEND  ⏎
      RETURN  ⏎
```

Solution:

The `Preparations:` section sets up two arrays, `Square%` and `Noise%`. These wave data arrays must have at least 255 elements.

The `MENU` statements define the menu bar and the two titles: **Program** (menu 1) and **Waveform** (menu 2). The second parameter in the `MENU` statement (0=menu name, 1-3=menu entry) and the third position can be either a 0, 1 or 2.

0 produces a ghost item; 1 produces a normal menu item; and 2 marks the menu item with a checkmark.

The next FOR...NEXT loop fulfills a number of parameters at once: It computes the contents of the waveform data arrays. The first 127 array elements of `Square%` receive the value 127 and the remaining elements receive -128. The amplitude can range from 127 to -128 for a pulse wave.

`Noise%` fills with random numbers for the white noise waveform.

The program draws horizontal lines on the screen, four pixels apart, to help with selecting notes and mouse movement.

The condition IF INT(x/4)=x/4 THEN... applies to any multiple of 4.

The third possible waveform (sine) appears automatically from AmigaBASIC from the WAVE 0,SIN statement. Sine waves aren't automatically created. The variable Wform states which of the three waveforms is active. This checkmark display in the pulldown menu shows the active waveform.

The program works with event trapping. Menu events operate through the program section `MenuControl:`, while `MouseControl:` handles mouse events.

`MainProgram:` consists of an endless loop.

The user calls `MenuControl:` when a menu item is selected. The variable `Men` contains the menu number, according to the BASIC function `MENU(0)`. This can be 1 when the selected item is in the **Program** menu, or 2 when found in the **Waveform** menu.

The variable `Item` gives the number of selectable options within the specified menu.

If `Men=1` and `Item=1`, the user selected the first item in the first menu, ending the program. The screen clears with `CLS` and the program stops at `END`.

The next block is a typical set of nested `IF...THEN` constructs. If the second menu is selected (`IF Men=2 THEN...`), you must reset the checkmark in the second menu. The first three program lines in the large `IF...THEN-ENDIF` structure means that the variable `Wform` contains the last active waveform option (this is set to 1 when the program starts). The third value in the `MENU` statement sets this menu item from 2 to 1. Then `Wform` becomes the selected menu item. This option is marked by a checkmark through `MENU 2,Wform,2` (the 2 in the third place is additional).

Then the program checks the selected item and sets it with `WAVE 0` and the waveform for voice 0. The `ELSEIF` command means: If the last condition is unfulfilled, then you should look for another condition.

Two `ENDIF`s close the `IF...THEN...ENDIF` loop.

`RETURN` closes the subroutine.

The `Mousecontrol:` variable `Mousevalue` reads `MOUSE(0)`. This BASIC function checks the current status of the mouse buttons. The following executes through `WHILE...WEND:`. As long as `Mousevalue` is less than 0, a negative number occurs (this means that the mouse button is pressed at the time), and a tone sounds with `SOUND`. The variable `Mousevalue` must also be read within the `WHILE...WEND` loop, since this recognizes whether the mouse buttons change or not.

The frequency used by the SOUND command comes from the vertical mouse position (MOUSE(2)). The formula gives values between 130 and 1200, which approximates the first four octaves of the Amiga's musical range. Sound duration is 1 (approximately 1/18 second), and the AmigaBASIC volume and channel parameters are used (volume=127, channel=0 [both left channels]).

The delay loop FOR d=1 to 90:NEXT supplies the sound duration in increments of 1/18 second. If the user holds the left mouse button down for 1/60 of a second, the note plays for 1/18 second. If the user holds the left mouse button down for 1.001 seconds, the note plays for 1 and 1/18 seconds.

Herby

3.10   Lotto program

Lotto programs are very popular in computer books for one good reason: A lottery program generates *random numbers*. These are numbers which appear at random. The last few sections have covered AmigaBASIC graphics and sound. This Lotto program does something simpler—six random numbers appear on the screen.

```
Preparations: ⏎
RANDOMIZE TIMER ⏎
DIM digits(49) ⏎
FOR x=1 TO 49 ⏎
digits(x)=0 ⏎
NEXT ⏎
 ⏎
Arraydesign: ⏎
 FOR x=1 TO 7 ⏎
  FOR y=1 TO 7 ⏎
   LOCATE (3*y),16+6*x ⏎
   PRINT x+7*(y-1) ⏎
   LINE (159+48*(x-1),8+24*(y-1))-
(159+48*x,8+24*y),1,b ⏎
  NEXT y ⏎
 NEXT x ⏎
 ⏎
Drawing: ⏎
 w=w+1 ⏎
  x=INT(7*RND)+1 ⏎
  y=INT(7*RND)+1 ⏎
  Occ=0 : colour=3 :IF Right=6 THEN
colour=2 ⏎
  IF digits(x+7*(y-1))=0 THEN ⏎
   PAINT (160+48*(x-1),9+24*(y-1)),
colour,1 ⏎
   SOUND (x+7*(y-1))*8+440,1 ⏎
   FOR delay=1 TO 50 : NEXT delay ⏎
   PAINT (160+48*(x-1),9+24*(y-1)),0,1 ⏎
   Occ=1 ⏎
  END IF ⏎
  IF Occ=1 AND w>10 THEN ⏎
   PAINT (160+48*(x-1),9+24*(y-1)),
colour,1 ⏎
    digits(x+7*(y-1))=1 ⏎
    IF Right=6 THEN digits(x+7*(y-1))=2 ⏎
    Right=Right+1:w=0 : Status=x+7*(y-1) ⏎
    SOUND (x+7*(y-1))*8+440,8 ⏎
```

```
      FOR delay=1 TO 4000 : NEXT delay  ↵
      END IF  ↵
         ↵
      IF Right <7 THEN Drawing  ↵
         ↵
Ending:  ↵
 LOCATE 1,1 : COLOR 3,0  ↵
 PRINT "The winning"  ↵
 PRINT "number of the week:"  ↵
 COLOR 1,0 : PRINT  ↵
 FOR x=1 TO 49  ↵
  IF digits(x)=1 THEN PRINT x  ↵
 NEXT x  ↵
 PRINT  ↵
 PRINT "Extra number:";  ↵
 PRINT Status  ↵
 PRINT : COLOR 3,0  ↵
 PRINT "GOOD LUCK!": COLOR 1,0  ↵
   ↵
```

4
AmigaDOS

4.   AmigaDOS

This chapter discusses diskettes and the general commands and programs used in communicating with diskettes.

It's not essential that you completely understand this chapter. If you want to program in AmigaBASIC or plan to access only commercial software, then you won't need to read this chapter. However, you may want to learn a few of the basic principles of diskette access. This helps you become more familiar with the computer and its processes.

DOS

The controlling program used in diskette access is the *disk operating system*, or *DOS* for short. Like the operating system in a computer, the DOS controls general housekeeping tasks for diskettes. AmigaDOS is the Amiga's disk operating system. You can operate AmigaDOS through the Command Line Interface (CLI) mentioned in Chapter 2.

The Workbench diskette contains a program named Shell. This is an enhanced version of the CLI. We will refer to the CLI in this book instead of the Command Line Interface.

We'll describe how to access the CLI in this chapter. We'll also show how to send commands to AmigaDOS and describe the AmigaDOS commands which you'll use most often for disk access.

When you see the ⏎ symbol, remember this is the ENTER or RETURN key. It signifies when you should press the ⏎ key. Program lines which must be on one line in AmigaBASIC may appear on two lines in this book. This symbol will clarify when you should press the ⏎ key.

4.1   CLI

The CLI is an Amiga user interface. The major difference between the Workbench and the CLI is that the CLI offers more complex dialogue between the user and the Amiga. You use only the keyboard and not the mouse while in the CLI. For example, instead of double clicking on an object, you type in the command and press the ⏎ key.

This section discusses only the most important AmigaDOS commands. If you wish to become better acquainted with AmigaDOS, see the *AmigaDOS Inside and Out* book from Abacus. Once you see some of the possibilities which the Amiga offers and as we discuss them, you may want to learn more about AmigaDOS.

•   Start your Amiga, if it isn't already on.

•   Double-click the Workbench diskette icon.

A number of diskette icons appear.

Opening the
Shell

Open the Shell from the Workbench diskette window by double-clicking on its icon. You could also double click on the CLI icon in the System drawer.

•   Double-click on the Shell (or CLI) icon.

In a moment a new window appears on the screen. It's named AmigaShell. Although Workbench 1.3 displays either New CLI or New Shell, we'll always refer to it as the AmigaShell window.

The AmigaShell window has most of the gadgets that other windows have: Sizing gadget, drag bar and front/back gadget.

•   Make the window as large as you can by clicking on the full size gadget. Workbench 1.3 users should drag the sizing gadget of the AmigaShell window down and to the right.

The CLI prompt is one of the most important differences between the AmigaBASIC windows and the CLI window. The > character appears whenever the CLI is awaiting input. The 1 preceding the > indicates that this is the first CLI window. Other characters, such as SYS:, may appear between the 1 and the > which signify the current disk or drawer. It's possible to open several CLI windows at the same time.

•   Enter the following into the AmigaShell window:

        newcli ⏎

NEWCLI

Another `AmigaShell` window opens. Note the `New CLI process x` (called `task` in Workbench 1.3) appears in this new window. The `x` is a number which represents the current task. This text scrolls off the top of the screen once the window fills with commands or data. The `CLI` offers multiple windows because the Amiga is multitasking (can perform several tasks simultaneously). Therefore, if you have two disk drives, you can display the *directory* (diskette contents) of the internal drive in one `CLI` window and the external drive's directory in another `CLI` window.

The number preceding the > character indicates the `CLI` window currently in use. In this section, however, we'll only need one window. Therefore, you'll need to close the second window.

• Enter the following into one of the `CLI` windows:

> endcli ⏎

ENDCLI

This command closes the `AmigaShell` window currently in use. You can type AmigaDOS commands in uppercase letters, lowercase letters or even a combination of the two. Filenames can also be entered in uppercase and lowercase.

• Resize the `CLI` window so that it occupies the full screen.

• Enter the following into the `AmigaShell` window:

> dir ⏎

DIR

`DIR` is the abbreviation for DIRectory. The directory is a list of the contents on the diskette. Since the disk drive contains a copy of the Workbench diskette, the display should appear similar to the following:

```
Trashcan (dir)
c (dir)
Prefs (dir)
System (dir)
L (dir)
devs (dir)
S (dir)
T (dir)
fonts (dir)
libs (dir)
Wbstartup (dir)
Utilities (dir)
. . . . . . .
```

The word `.backdrop` (`.info` in Workbench 1.3) appears immediately after these names, then other filenames appear which list the contents, or directory, of the diskette. You should recognize by now many of the names displayed in this directory. For example,

Utilities was the name of a drawer in the Workbench diskette window.

You can easily open this drawer and read the files inside it from the CLI.

* Type the following:

    dir System ⏎

By requesting the directory of the System drawer, you call a *subdirectory*. This is actually a directory of a directory. The Amiga displays the names of the utility programs in two columns: Once under the names which they were saved and once followed by a suffix .info.

You can start some programs from the AmigaShell. The program doesn't even need to be in the subdirectory. As an example, let's try to start the Clock program.

* Type the following:

    clock ⏎

Running programs from the CLI

In a moment the clock program is loaded and the clock face appears on the screen. How did the Amiga find the clock program since it was not listed in the System directory?

The clock program is in the Utilities drawer (subdirectory). The Amiga was able to find the path to the clock program because it knew the path to the program.

* Type the following:

    path ⏎

This CLI command lists the current paths that the Amiga will use when searching for programs. These paths were setup when you started your Amiga. For more information on paths see *Amiga DOS Inside and Out* from Abacus.

When a program is in a drawer that is not part of the path you must specify the program and the subdirectory or subdirectories. From Chapter 3 you should remember that a slash (/) specifies the subdirectory in addition to the filename when saving a BASIC program (SAVE drawer/program_name). This is the same with the CLI, to access a program in a drawer, you must specify the program name and the drawer containing that program.

* Type the following:

    System/clock ⏎

This executes the clock program again. This time you specified the correct path. Until now, the only difference from opening programs from the Workbench is that you must type in the filename from the keyboard. As we've seen, the CLI has no icons. The advantage of CLI commands lies in letting you view any file, directory or subdirectory.

- Click on the Clock window's back gadget.

You cannot access the AmigaShell window when the Clock program is running. The CLI ignores any commands which you enter. This is because any program started from the CLI occupies the CLI during program execution. To avoid this, you can open another window beforehand, or enter a special command to make your Amiga do the extra work (multitasking):

- Click on the CLI window's back gadget.

- Click on the Clock window's close gadget.

- Type the following:

      run clock ⏎

The Amiga starts another task (CLI x) and runs Clock in that window. Your original CLI remains active as the Clock runs.

The biggest advantage of using CLI is having complete control over your Amiga.

You can return to the main directory from a subdirectory by using the slash and CD:

      cd / ⏎

We'll explain this command in more detail in the next section.

Workbench
1.3 only

Workbench 1.3 users can also see and work with all the files on a diskette. Workbench 2.0 users can use a menu selection to view all the files on their diskettes and can even execute CLI commands directly from the **Workbench** menu.

The directory c, which appeared after the dir command above, wasn't in the Workbench 1.3 diskette window. However, the Amiga uses many CLI commands so a directory for them, named c, is on the Workbench diskette.

- Type the following:

      dir c ⏎

The CLI command names appear on the screen. These commands are accessed thru the CLI and more commands can be added to your Amiga.

4.2   Amiga diskettes

You can consider each Amiga diskette as a type of filing cabinet. The cabinet contains drawers, the drawers contain files and the files contain data. Diskette operations often take place with several diskettes and not just one. The Amiga tries managing these as quickly and as carefully as possible. To permit this with a large amount of data, a *hierarchy* exists in AmigaDOS. A hierarchy is a certain order for stacking programs or information on diskette.

For example, say a program wants to find out what the font Sapphire 19 looks like. The following is the process it would take:

The Amiga receives the message that the Sapphire 19 font is required. AmigaDOS then searches for a drawer labeled fonts. If there is no such drawer, then the Amiga has the wrong diskette and tells the user with a requester.

AmigaDOS finds and opens the fonts drawer. Inside are several files. The Amiga then searches until it finds the drawer named Sapphire. The Amiga opens the Sapphire drawer and searches for the file named 19. Once found, the Amiga gives the program the desired information and closes the file. The Amiga turns to other tasks again until it receives a new inquiry.

You can also do this from the CLI with the following commands:

* Type the following:

    dir fonts ⏎

    dir fonts/sapphire ⏎

You read the names of available drawers. Then you opened the fonts drawer to see what was inside. You selected the Sapphire font file and read the names of the two Sapphire font sizes.

Perhaps Sapphire has no more sizes and opening the file reveals all that it contains. How do you find out whether more data exists in the Sapphire file?

Suffixes

Notice these words follow some of the names in a directory:

    .info   (dir)

These are *suffixes*. These suffixes help the Amiga determine the function of a specific file. All files with the suffix `.info` contain data corresponding to the filename preceding the suffix.

Therefore, the file `Clock.info` provides the Amiga with all the data required to display the Clock icon and write the name Clock in the `Workbench` window.

It's rarely necessary to specify a suffix when calling a given file from the `CLI`. However, files with suffixes can also be read. For example, consider the suffix `(dir)`. All names with this suffix are subdirectories and not programs.

• Type the following:

    dir ⏎

The Amiga displays a list of all the directories and files on the diskette. Take another look at the `System` directory.

• Type the following:

    dir system ⏎

info

The Amiga displays `.info` followed by the program names. Those names followed by the `.info` suffix are viewable as icons on the Workbench. These are the icons that are viewable when the `Show/Only Icons` submenu item is selected from the **Windows** menu in Workbench 2.0. Any names not followed by `.info` are not seen as normal icons on the Workbench. Take a look at the Fonts directory.

• Type the following:

    dir fonts ⏎

As the font names appear, notice that each name has a `(dir)` following it. This means that each font has additional files enclosed. Remember how to access this from the example in the previous section?

• Type the following:

    dir fonts/diamond ⏎

This displays the subdirectory of the `diamond` font directory. There are no other subdirectories. The subdirectory probably displays only the 12 and 20 font sizes. You'll note that these fonts have no `.info` files. Without an `.info` file, a file remains invisible to the Workbench.

It obviously takes time to enter all these commands for directories, subdirectories and sub-subdirectories. Also, when a second disk drive or the RAM disk is marked for access you must supply the *drive specifier*.

For example, to read the second disk drive's directory from the CLI, you enter:

    dir df1:

For a RAM disk, the directory access is as follows:

    dir ram:

CD

The CD command represents Change Directory. It saves most of this typing. CD allows you to change the second drive to the default drive or a specific directory to the default directory. Normally when you enter dir, the Amiga displays a main directory. CD changes the specified directory into the default directory.

*   Type the following:

    cd utilities ⏎

The disk drive runs briefly.

*   Type the following:

    dir ⏎

The Amiga displays the subdirectory utilities instead of the main directory. Now you can start a program directly.

*   Type the following:

    calculator ⏎

The program promptly starts without you specifying the utilities first. However, if you now want to start a program located in the main directory, the Amiga won't be able to find it. This is because the CLI is still in the demos directory.

*   Click on the Calculator window's close gadget.

Here's a way to see everything on a diskette. You must be in the main directory to view the entire diskette. Before you continue, you need two additional CD options.

*   Type the following:

    cd ⏎

As soon as you press the ⏎ key, the message Workbench 2.0:Utilities appears. Additional messages will appear depending on how far into the directory you move. For example, if you're in the Sapphire subdirectory of the Fonts directory of the Workbench 1.3 diskette, the message following the CD command reads:

Workbench 2.0:Fonts/Sapphire

CD /

This CD command variation returns you to the next directory up (you must put a space between the CD and the slash):

cd / ⏎

CD:

The CD: command takes you directly to the main directory (again, include a space between the CD and the colon).

If you're in the main directory, the command below displays the entire contents of the disk directory.

• Type the following:

cd: ⏎

• Type the following:

dir opt a ⏎

Each directory name appears, followed by its files and subdirectories. You can stop the names from scrolling off the top of the screen by pressing the [Spacebar] and continue the scrolling by pressing the ⏎ (Backspace) key. Continue in this way until you have reached the font you want.

You may be wondering why you don't always see all these filenames as icons in the Workbench window. Consider what would happen if the CLI displayed everything. You may never use all of these options. Most of them supply information to programs and don't require icons. Only data required by the user is visible. Anything else only leads to confusion, which is why most of these names stay unseen by Intuition.

LIST

LIST is a very comprehensive command and features several options. We'll show you the three most important parameters.

• Type the following:

list ⏎

LIST alone results in a sorted list of names and characters. If the top line is about to scroll off the top of the screen, press the [Spacebar] to pause the listing. Pressing the ⏎ key continues the listing.

A number of names and characters follow. Here are two sample LIST entries:

```
Clock          19596 ---rwed  03-Feb-90  08:57:36
Fonts            Dir ---rwed  03-Feb-90  09:02:28
```

The first item is the name of the program or file. The number following the filename indicates the file's length in bytes. For example, `Clock`, with 19596 bytes, is one of the longest programs on the Workbench diskette.

Note that `Fonts` has the word `Dir` and no numbers. This is because directories have no lengths. They exist to keep files in order. You can always tell at a glance whether an entry is a program or a directory. The entry "empty" may also replace the byte size or the `Dir` entry. This means that a program contains no data.

The next item specifies the program's file status (`rwed`=Read/ Write/ Execute/ Deleteable). This item shows whether the file can be read (`r`), whether the user can write to it (`w`), whether the file can be run or executed (`e`) and whether the file can be deleted (`d`).

You can specify all these options in the `Information` window and access them from the Workbench screen.

LIST DATE

The date and time display refer to when you created or changed the file. The day listed refers to the most recent day. For example, Thursday refers to the most recent Thursday. AmigaDOS always calculates and displays the dates up to the previous week. The number of files or programs processed in the last week determine the number of files labeled with a specific day, for example Thursday.

`LIST` provides other parameters to display the exact date.

• Type the following:

    list dates ⏎

This displays all the files with their dates and the actual day if the file was created in the last week. Therefore, you can quickly find the date of a particular version or file.

LIST SINCE

To simplify finding out "What I did when" you can specify dates to the Amiga from and/or up until you wish to see all the files.

• Type the following:

    list since 23-apr-88 ⏎

Make certain to include the - character. The date must appear in the same format as the `List` display.

This displays lists only the files created or edited from April 23, 1988 to today's date. The number of program names appearing depends on how much or how little was stored on the Workbench since the 23th of April 1988. The actual dates on which these program names were written won't appear.

- Type the following:

  `list since thursday ⏎`

The Amiga automatically displays everything stored since the previous Thursday. If nothing was stored since Thursday, then the 1> prompt reappears.

There is also a special option for finding out everything stored before a given date.

LIST UP TO

- Type the following:

  `list upto 24-apr-88 ⏎`

Make certain not to have a space between "upto". Now the Amiga displays everything entered on the diskette prior to this date. Therefore, LIST offers a wide range of options for scanning through files according to given criteria. This option is available using a CLI command. There is no facility in the Workbench menus for determining the date or time of the data stored.

One more point about using UPTO and SINCE. You must enter single-digit dates (e.g., 1 January) as two digits (e.g., 1 becomes 01). Otherwise, the Amiga ignores the UPTO or SINCE commands.

NOTE:

If you have memory expansion for your Amiga 500, you also own a battery operated clock. This clock is not set in the factory, so if no one else has already set it for you, it's probably wrong. To see if its correct do the following:

- Enter the CLI command:

  `date ⏎`

- If the date and time are correct, your system clock is set correctly. You'll have to enter the date and time in the same format displayed by your Amiga:

  day, month, year, hour, minute and second
  DD-MM-YY HH:MM:SS

- To set the date, enter the following CLI command but substitute the correct date and time. Notice that format of the date and the month is specified by a three letter abbreviation.

  `date 20-MAR-90 12:30:00 ⏎`

- Then enter the CLI command:

  `setclock save ⏎`

RENAME

The RENAME command is another important CLI command. RENAME has two functions. Its primary function is to rename files.

For example, say you want to change one font to another name.

- Type the following:

  cd fonts ⏎
  rename ruby.font to luby.font ⏎

- You can confirm that the font has the new name by typing the following:

  dir ⏎

The font name Ruby is now Luby.

- Type the following:

  rename luby to ruby ⏎
  cd : ⏎

The closing cd: changes the original directory to the default directory.

The second function for RENAME is to transfer programs and files to another directory.

- Type the following:

  dir utilities ⏎
  rename utilities/clock to trashcan/notepad ⏎
  rename utilities/clock.info to trashcan/clock.info ⏎
  dir demos ⏎

The Clock moves from the Utilities directory.

- Type the following:

  dir trashcan ⏎

You can use RENAME to rename programs and files and then transfer them from one directory to another.

- Use the sizing gadget to reduce the CLI window as much as possible.

- Double-click the Utilities drawer from the Workbench diskette window.

- Double-click the Trashcan icon.

As you can see, the `Clock` program went from the `Utilities` drawer to the `Trashcan` icon. You can put everything back again without re-entering the `CLI`.

• Using the mouse pointer, drag the `Clock` icon from the `Trashcan` window back to the `Utilities` window.

Now you are familiar with a few of the AmigaDOS commands and you have some insight into the number of programs operating in the background handling windows, pointers and menus.

4.3   CLI tricks and tips

The CLI allows you to do some things that are impossible through the Workbench alone. One example is that you can only copy larger and more complex programs through the CLI.

One of these programs is the printer driver. The Extras diskette contains several additional printer drivers. If you need one of these programs, there are instructions below for copying it to your Workbench.

Second, the CLI can help single drive owners get around some tight situations when dealing with the CLI. These problems arise because the Amiga must access all CLI commands from a diskette as needed. You can solve the diskette switching problem using a short DOS program called a *batch file* (more on this in a moment).

Third, when you work with BASIC, single drive system owners would find it much more convenient to have a *bootable* BASIC diskette. A bootable BASIC diskette contains a copy of the Workbench, along with the program material you need.

If you find the material below useful, or you find that you enjoy working with the CLI more than anything else so far, you can find more extensive information in the Abacus book *Amiga Tricks and Tips*.

Printer drivers   If you tried selecting a printer driver from the Printer program in Preferences (Change Printer screen of Preferences in Workbench 1.3) and didn't find your printer, use the CLI to look in the devs/printers drawer on the Extras diskette. There are more printer drivers on that diskette.

If you find your printer listed there, here's how to copy your particular printer driver to the Workbench.

NOTE: There are some rules you should follow when performing the procedure listed below:

> Perform the following operation with backup copies ONLY of the Workbench and Extras diskettes. You may erase files which you may need at a later time. Delete only from and copy only to your backups.

> This operation requires a large amount of memory. If you own a 256K Amiga 1000 in particular, be sure that no extra windows are open and that absolutely no programs are running in the background.

Make sure you know the exact name of your Extras diskette. Better yet, RENAME and label the Extras diskette Extrasd (if its name is different).

NOTE: Most printers work under the Epson driver. Use that driver if your printer doesn't appear in the Extras diskette printer driver list.

- Insert the Workbench diskette in the disk drive.

- Close all windows and make sure no extra programs are running.

- Double-click on the Workbench diskette icon.

- Double-click on the Shell icon.

- Enter the following:

  cd devs/printers ⏎
  dir ⏎

A group of printer names appears. They are the same ones found in Printer program in Preferences. Now you can use the CLI delete command to delete the printer drivers you won't need.

- For example, if you won't need to use the Okidata 292 printer, type the following:

  delete OKIDATA_292 ⏎

This deletes the Okidata 292 printer driver from this file.

- Delete the printer drivers which you do need need and keep only those which you will use.

The following command must use the name of your Extras diskette. Therefore, use your Extras diskette name if you're not using Extrasd. The best bet is to rename your Extras diskette to Extrasd to avoid confusion.

- Enter the following:

  cd extrasd:devs/printers

Remember the colon following extrasd. The Amiga requests the Extras diskette.

- Insert the Extras diskette and enter:

  copy #? to ram:

- Insert the Workbench diskette when the Amiga prompts you for it.

Again, remember the colon following `ram`. The `#?` symbol is called a *wildcard*. This particular wildcard tells the operating system to copy every directory entry from the `Extras` diskette to the RAM disk.

- Insert the `Extras` diskette when the Amiga prompts you for it.

As the Amiga copies the printer driver to the RAM disk the filename is displayed in the window.

- When the Amiga is ready, enter:

  `cd ram:` ⏎

- Remove the `Extras` diskette and insert the `Workbench` diskette when the appropriate requester appears.

Now copy the printer driver from the RAM disk to the Workbench.

- Type the following:

  `copy ram:(printername) to df0:devs/printers`
  ⏎

- Insert your printer name for `(printername)`.

- When the process finishes, enter:

  `dir df0:devs/printers` ⏎

You'll see your printer driver in the disk directory of the Amiga's internal drive.

- Delete the RAM disk by entering:

  `delete ram:#?` ⏎

WARNING: Before you press the ⏎ key, make absolutely sure that this command reads exactly as it appears here. Otherwise, the wildcard instructs the Amiga to delete all the entries in the directory most recently accessed (the diskette in drive `df0:`).

- Install your printer driver using the `printer` program of `Preferences`.

Fonts

The Amiga has the ability to display multiple fonts which greatly enhances its capabilities. The `Extras` diskette contains fonts that work with a *Page Description Language* called Postscript. This is one of the many system upgrades that was made from Workbench 1.2 to 1.3. Workbench 1.2 users will not have these fonts, but this upgrade only requires a disk for the Amiga instead of expensive hardware.

The advantage of a Page Description language is that it is device independent, which means the Postscript output can be sent to a wide variety of printers and photo-typesetters. This book was printed using Postscript with the same fonts that are available on the Extras 1.3 diskette: Times, `Courier` and Helvetica. To access the fonts they must be on the Workbench diskette. Use the `CLI` to look in the `devs/fonts` drawer on the `Extras` diskette. This is where the postscript fonts are located. Since you can also purchase and add fonts to your Amiga system, your Amiga is truly an ever expanding system.

Here's how to copy the new Postscript fonts to the Workbench.

NOTE:

There are some rules you should follow when performing the procedure listed below:

Perform the following operation with backup copies ONLY of the `Workbench` and `Extras` diskettes. You may erase files which you may need at a later time. Delete only from and copy only to your backups.

This operation requires a great deal of disk space so delete as many printer drivers and utility programs (Calculator, Say, More, GraphicDump, etc.) as possible from the `Workbench` diskette to make room for the fonts.

Make sure you know the exact name of your `Extras` diskette. Better yet, RENAME and label the `Extras` diskette `Extrasd` (if its name is different).

NOTE:

To make room on our Workbench diskette we deleted the `Clock`, all the programs from the `Utilities` drawer and every printer driver except `Epson` and `generic` from the `devs/printers` drawer.

Delete the programs from the `Utilities` drawer of the `Workbench` diskette. Make sure it's a copy – NOT THE ORIGINAL. Follow the previous directions for printer drivers to delete the unnecessary printer drivers.

The following command must use the name of your `Extras` diskette. If you have a different name than `Extrasd`, use that name. The best bet is to rename your `Extras` diskette to `Extrasd` to avoid confusion.

• Enter the following:

cd extrasd: ⏎

Remember the colon following extrasd. The Amiga requests the Extras diskette.

- Insert the Extras diskette and enter:

    copy fonts to ram:fonts all ⏎

- When the Amiga asks, insert the Workbench diskette.

Again, remember the colon following ram. Fonts specifies the name of the drawer and all tells the operating system to copy everything in the fonts drawer to the RAM disk.

- Insert the Extras diskette when the appropriate requester appears.

As the Amiga copies the fonts to the RAM disk the font name is displayed in the window.

- When the Amiga is ready, enter:

    cd ram: ⏎

- Remove the Extrasd diskette and insert the Workbench diskette when the appropriate requester appears.

Now copy the fonts from the RAM disk to the Workbench.

- Type the following:

    copy ram:fonts to df0:fonts all ⏎

- When the process finishes, enter:

    dir df0:fonts ⏎

You'll see the new fonts in the disk directory of the Amiga's internal drive.

- Delete the fonts from the RAM disk by entering:

    delete ram:fonts all ⏎

- Workbench 1.3 users should run the fixfonts program by entering:

    fixfonts ⏎

WARNING: Before you press the ⏎ key, make absolutely sure that this command reads exactly as it appears here. Otherwise, the all instructs the Amiga to delete all the entries in the directory most recently accessed (the diskette in drive df0:).

Load the font program from the Prefs drawer and select the various fonts to actually see what the new fonts look like. Workbench 1.3 users will have to load the Notepad program and select the font menu to actually see what the new fonts look like.

International Amiga

The Amiga is an international computer and rather than create a different Amiga for each country the Amiga designers decided on a different approach. They would load the correct keyboard driver, or keymap into the Amiga when it is turned on. The early copies of Workbench contained these keymaps in the devs/keymaps directory. Due to space limitations on the later editions of the Workbench diskette they were moved to the Extras diskette. The Extras diskette contains the foreign language keymaps in the devs/keymaps directory. They are loaded with the SetMap program in the System drawer.

The keymaps are named after the letters for the countries used on international auto license plates. The following keymaps are available on the Extras diskette or the Workbench diskette in the devs/keymaps directory:

cdn	Canadian
ch1	Swiss 1
ch2	Swiss 2
d	German
dk	Danish
e	Spanish
f	French
gb	Great Britain
i	Italian
is	Islandic
n	Norwegian
s	Swedish/Finnish
usa0	USA0
usa1	USA1
usa2	USA2

To examine the different keymaps they can be loaded directly, if the correct path is specified. The following example requires the Workbench diskette in drive df0: and the Extras diskette in drive df1, enter:

```
system/setmap df1:devs/keymaps/d⏎ (1.3 &
2.0)
system/setmap df0:devs/keymaps/d⏎ (1.2)
```

This will load the German (Deutsch) keyboard. Workbench 1.3 users can examine the new keyboard layout by loading the KeyToy 2000 program in the Tools drawer of the Extras diskette. Other Workbench users may load the Shell and try the different keys (Y, Z & ;) to see the difference.

To return to the original US keymap enter:

```
setmap usa1 ⏎
```

The keymaps can be copied to your Workbench diskette in the same manner as the fonts were copied.

The following commands must use the name of your Extras diskette. If you have a different name than Extrasd, use that name. The best bet is to rename your Extras diskette to Extrasd to avoid confusion.

* Enter the following:

```
cd extrasd: ⏎
```

* Insert the Extras diskette when prompted. Then enter:

```
copy devs/keymaps to ram: all ⏎
```

* When the Amiga asks, insert the Workbench diskette.

Again, remember the colon following ram. Devs/keymaps specifies the name of the drawer and all tells the operating system to copy everything in the keymaps drawer to the RAM disk.

* Insert the Extras diskette when the appropriate requester appears.

As the Amiga copies the keymaps to the RAM disk the keymap name is displayed in the CLI window.

* When the Amiga is ready, enter:

```
cd ram: ⏎
```

* Remove the Extrasd diskette and insert the Workbench diskette when the appropriate requester appears.

Now load a new keymap.

* Type the following:

```
copy ram:d to df0:devs/keymaps ⏎
```

This copies a new keymap (German-Deutsch) to the correct directory, if you wish to use another keymap it should be copied to the devs/keymaps directory.

You can also load the keymaps directly on startup by altering the startup-sequence. The keymaps must be copied to the devs/keymaps drawer on the Workbench diskette and then loaded with the SetMap program in the startup-sequence.

Appendices

Appendices

These Appendices contain information you may not find elsewhere in this book.

Appendix A is a short course in troubleshooting your Amiga. Most of these solutions apply to your first time assembling and turning on your Amiga. The problems consist of the little things that can go wrong when your starting out.

Appendix B is a list of terms. Most of these terms already appeared in the book, and may need more explanation. There are also words here that didn't appear in the book at all, and are listed here with definitions for later reference.

Appendix C offers instructions for using `IconEd` in Workbench 2.0. You'll use `IconEd` (icon editor) for creating your own icons or editing the icons that already exist on your diskettes.

Appendix D offers instructions for using `IconEd` in Workbench 1.3.

Appendix E contains a few general technical notes about the Amiga and its internal features (circuitry, video and sound, etc.).

A: First Aid

Problem: No screen display.

Solution: There could be several reasons for this. You have forgotten to plug the
                 monitor into the wall socket, or you didn't connect the monitor to the
                 computer. If your using the Amiga monitor (i.e., the Commodore RGB
                 monitor), make sure that the VIDEO MODE switch under the door is
                 switched to **RGB**. The switch should be in the far right position. This
                 could also happen on other RGB monitors.

Problem: No sound.

Solution: First, check the volume control on your monitor; it may be all the way
                 off. Second, make sure that the Amiga sound output is connected to a
                 monitor or stereo system (see Section 1.1 of this book for connecting
                 instructions).

Problem: The BASIC window, CLI and Notepad reject any input.

Solution: This most often occurs when you run a BASIC program and click the
                 pointer on the LIST window. Now you can't enter any data in the
                 BASIC window until you click on the BASIC window again.

                 This fault can also occur on the Amiga 1000 or 2000 if the keyboard
                 cable becomes disconnected.

Problem: Computer ignores mouse input.

Solution: Be sure your mouse is plugged into JOYSTICK 1. If the mouse still
                 doesn't work, open the mouse and make sure that the mouse's ball
                 moves freely. You may need to open the mouse to free up the ball (see
                 Section 1.2 for instructions on opening the mouse).

Problem: Newly formatted diskette window's disk gauge says that the diskette is
                 full.

Solution: If the disk gauge says that the diskette is full, and you just copied or
                 formatted it, or it only contains a few files, then you're in trouble. You
                 probably removed the diskette from the drive while the disk drive LCD
                 was still on. That act destroys diskette data. The only way to make the
                 diskette usable again is to reformat it (see the section on the System
                 drawer for instructions on formatting). You might be able to recover
                 some of the files using the diskdoctor from the CLI (see the next
                 Solution).

Problem: READ/WRITE ERROR displayed on screen.

Solution: Occasionally disks may not be running at top efficiency. This is when READ/WRITE ERRORS occur. That is, the Amiga can no longer access the diskette. One day a diskette may load fine, the next it may not ever work again. There are some ways around this problem.

• Format a blank diskette.

• If you only have one disk drive, copy directory c over to the RAM disk.

• Start the CLI and enter:

        diskdoctor df0:¶

The Amiga tells you which track has the problem, then attempts to recover the files on that track.

• When the diskdoctor finishes, it requests that you COPY NECESSARY FILES TO NEW DISK. Enter:

        copy df0:#? to empty: all

Replace the name empty with your own diskette name. This target diskette must be empty.

Problem: Accidentally deleted programs.

Solution: This happens frequently: You accidentally delete something you didn't want to delete. It doesn't matter whether you do this from the Workbench or from the CLI. Don't save anything else to that diskette right now, or else you might overwrite the deleted program.

• Go to the CLI and activate the diskdoctor.

• After the diskdoctor finishes, enter:

        dir¶

Your missing files may or may not be in the directory.

• Enter the following to exit the CLI:

        endcli¶

Problem: Keys repeat too fast.

Solution: Adjust the key repeat rate in Preferences (see Section 2.10 for instructions).

Problem: Text display is unreadable.

Solution: You can also solve this by using the wbscreen program in the Prefs drawer. Workbench 1.3 users should use the Preferences program. Certain color combinations make text unreadable (white on white, for example). If this occurs click on the Reset All gadget. This changes the Amiga back to its original Workbench colors. If this problem occurs in BASIC, restart the program. The screen values reset at the beginning of every BASIC program. As soon as the program restarts, stop the program by selecting the Stop item from the **Run** pulldown menu. Remember to correct the program before you run it again.

Problem: Icons appear out of nowhere.

Solution: Sometimes, especially just after programming in BASIC, a program icon which should be in the BASICDemos drawer appears in the Workbench diskette window instead. You must specify exactly where this program should be saved. To return the icon where it belongs, drag the icon to the correct drawer or diskette icon.

Problem: Files disappear.

Solution: The program may be stored in the wrong drawer. Look through all the drawers and windows. If you still haven't found the program, you've managed to bypass all the built-in safety features of the Amiga, and erased the program without saving it.

Problem: Program constantly produces software errors.

Solution: Software errors can be caused by almost anything within a program. There's one problem, however, that often can be solved by the user. Some programs cannot run on an Amiga with more than 512K of memory. If you have memory expansion going above 512K, double-click the NoFastMem icon in the System drawer before running the problem program. This cuts the additional memory off, allowing the program to run properly. If this still doesn't work, contact the software manufacturer or dealer and ask about updates or error reports for the program. After all, it's possible that other people have encountered the same problem, and that it has been resolved in the meantime.

Problem: Problems not mentioned above.

Solution: See your dealer. First try to determine whether it is a hardware or software failure. For example, if the Amiga constantly rejects the Workbench diskette, the fault probably lies in the software. Take the diskette to the dealer. Only visit the dealer when all else fails.

B: Computer Glossary

Alert
This is a type of requester that appears at the top of the screen when the Amiga has a major error. Alerts display in red, with a blinking border, red lettering and a black background. Follow the Amiga's instructions to get out of it (see also *Guru meditation*).

ASCII
Acronym for American Standard Code for Information Interchange. ASCII is the standard for keyboard character codes, which applies to some extent to keyboards and printers. The ASCII standard covers key codes 0 to 127; individual computer manufacturers assign their own characters to codes 128 to 255.

Assembler
An assembler lets you enter and run programs in *machine language*. Machine language is quicker than BASIC because there is no need to translate the command through an *interpreter* (see *BASIC interpreter*). However, machine language is very difficult to learn.

Backup copy
Duplicate of an original disk or file. Making backup copies is a good habit to develop. Data on a disk can easily and accidentally be destroyed.

BASIC interpreter
This program continuously runs in the computer once you load AmigaBASIC. It enables the computer to interpret and execute commands entered by a user in the BASIC language.

BASIC Language
A programming language (Beginner's All-purpose Symbolic Instruction Code). BASIC is popular with users as a computer language because it is easy to learn. Many manufacturers include an implementation of BASIC (such as AmigaBASIC) when you purchase a computer.

Baud
The unit used to measure the rate of data transmission, for example when communicating with another computer by telephone. A baud is approximately 1 bit per second. The term comes from J.M.E. Baudot, the inventor of the Baudot telegraph code, and was originally designed to describe the transmission capabilities of telegraph facilities.

In modern terms, the baud rate is the number of signal events (the signal for a 1 bit and the signal for a 0 bit are both "events") that take place on a telecommunications line each second. Standard baud rates include 300 baud, 1200 baud, 2400 baud, etc.

Binary   A number system consisting of only two numbers (0,1), sometimes called bits. Unlike the decimal number system with its 10 numbers (0-9), the binary number system is better suited to the internal structure of a computer. Just as larger numbers can be composed in the decimal system, larger binary system numbers are constructed from several digits. Both number systems rely on the positional value of numbers. The numbers 0 - 9 in the 10 to the 0 power column have the value 0 - 9. The same numbers in the next column (10 to the 1 power) refer to 10 - 90, etc. In the binary system the column value increases as follows: 0, 2, 4, 8, 16, 32, etc.

Bit   Bit is an abbreviation for BInary digiT. This is the smallest data unit a computer can process. It can only assume two states (0,1) and therefore store only two different pieces of information. This reduces the likelihood of data transmission errors. To store a character, several bits must be combined into a byte. Eight bits equal 1 *byte*. See also *Binary*.

Block   Memory on diskette is measured in blocks. For example, a file of about 543 bytes in length takes up about 2 blocks on diskette. Blocks appear in `Information` windows.

Bus   A collection of communication lines transmitting signals between components on a circuit board or between the circuit board and expansion or other cards.

Byte   A group of eight bits. Every memory cell in the Amiga consists of one byte (eight bits). The highest figure a byte can represent is 255, since 255 in the binary number system = 11111111. Therefore a byte can store up to 255 different characters.

               A byte can also represent a letter or character. The internal memory capacity of the Amiga 500 comprises a maximum of 524,288 such characters.

C   C is another programming language. Although it's a very fast executing language, it's very hard to learn. However, once mastered, C offers the user no end of opportunities on the Amiga.

CAD   CAD represents Computer Aided Design. This process speeds up the design aspects of many fields, from architecture to auto manufacturing.

Central   The most common use of this term refers to the main *chip* of a
processing   computer (for example, the 68000 microprocessor in the Amiga). This
unit   book uses *central processing unit* to describe the Amiga itself.

Centronics   Standard connection between a printer and your Amiga. The connection
                    of other devices to the Amiga occurs through interfaces. These
                    interfaces use standardized connectors. There are serial interfaces, in
                    which data is sent as individual bits, and parallel interfaces, in which a
                    byte can be transmitted simultaneously. Both interfaces have their own
                    standards: Centronics interfaces for parallel; RS-232 interfaces for
                    serial. Most printers are attached through the parallel Centronics
                    interface.

Chips   Complicated electronic circuitry built into a small space. The early days
                    of electronics required huge circuits. Chips compressed this same
                    circuitry into a single silicon chip, and made it possible to develop
                    small computers for the home.

                    Everything in the computer depends on the chips. Each chip contains
                    hundreds of electronic circuits. These circuits control the sound, graphic
                    and logic systems of the Amiga.

Cinch cable   The Amiga has 2 cinch outputs for connecting its audio output to
                    stereo equipment. Another term for cinch cable is *RCA cable*.

CLI   Stands for Command Line Interface. This is an all text interface that
                    can greatly enhance your work with the Amiga.

Cold start   Switching the computer off and on. Unlike the warm start, the cold
                    start is the complete turning off and turning back on of the computer.
                    The cold start is the last chance to have the computer start completely
                    new. Since switching the computer off and on adds stress to the
                    electronic components, use the warm start ($\boxed{\text{Ctrl}}$ <Commodore logo>
                    (or left <Amiga>) right <Amiga>) whenever possible.

Compatible   Something is compatible if it operates or agrees with something else.
                    If your printer works with the Amiga, then it's compatible. If your hard
                    disk doesn't work with your Amiga, it's incompatible.

Computer   Computers simulate animation by continually erasing and redisplaying
animation   dots on the screen. This is best explained in the animation demo in
                    Section 3.7. The quality of the animation depends on the speed of the
                    computer and the quality of the picture.

CPU   Abbreviation for Central Processing Unit. This is the main
                    microprocessor of the Amiga; sometimes used to describe the Amiga's
                    case as well.

Current   To access a file or a directory, DOS uses the current directory. You can
directory   make the directory current by using the CLI and AmigaShell window.
                    Type either CD : or CD NAME command.

Current drive	The standard drive or current drive is the drive to which all disk commands of the computer apply. Usually, and especially for systems with only one drive, this is DF0:. If two drives are available, the second drive can be selected with DF1: or DF2:.
Cursor	The cursor is an entry marker. Different cursors appear on the Amiga screen, according to whether you are programming in BASIC or entering DOS commands. The Amiga system also has the mouse pointer (the arrow moved by the mouse).
Databus	A line used to transmit data between the CPU and RAM or ROM memory.
Data transfer rate	The rate that data is transferred from a computer to a disk drive or from one computer to another computer.
Destination disk	It's the disk which is to receive data during the backup procedure. When copying data from one disk to another, the disk being copied is the source disk and the target disk is the disk receiving data.
Device driver	A subprogram to control communications between the computer and a peripheral.
DIP switch	A series of small switches used by computers and peripherals to configure the equipment.
DIR	Amiga command in the AmigaShell to display the directory of the disk which is in the current drive.
Directory	Part of a storage medium. Before the hard disk drive was commonly used, all files were stored in one directory, the root directory. Because of the large capacity of the hard disk drive, a separation into various directories became necessary. They are arranged in a tree structure where the root directory can contain files and subdirectories. Every subdirectory in turn can contain files and subdirectories.
Diskette	Diskettes are small plastic boxes containing magnetic media. This magnetic media holds data placed on it by a disk drive, and can be recalled by the Amiga at any time.
DOS	Short for *disk operating system*. This is the program which controls all operations between the computer and the disk drives. It has its own interpreter which allows you to enter commands directly from the keyboard. The Amiga's DOS is accessible through the CLI.
Editing	Editing is the process of changing text or program code within the computer. For example, you can edit either a program or the mouse pointer from Preferences.
Empty directory	A directory containing no files or subdirectories.

Expansion port	This is the external computer connector which permits adding memory and peripherals.
File	Data stored under a name assigned by the user or manufacturer. Data files (for example programs, text, graphics, etc.) appear in the directory of a disk or hard disk drive as an entry containing the name, extension, size and date of storage.
Filename	A group of letters and numbers indicating a specific file stored in a directory. A filename consists of the filename itself and the extension.
Format	Formatting a disk prepares to store data by dividing the disk into different sections. Be careful when using the Format item because it erases all the data and information on the diskette.
Guru meditation	When the Amiga stops working because of software problems, system crashes (see Section 2.5) etc., an *alert* appears at the top of the screen, calling the error a `Guru Meditation`. There's nothing you can do about this when it happens; just follow the instructions in the alert.
Hardware	The computer, internal chips and the keyboard are considered hardware. Printers and external disk drives are also called hardware, but are usually referred to as peripherals.
Hertz (Hz)	A unit of measure which equals a frequency of one cycle per second.
Initialization	Another term for the process of formatting a diskette or hard drive so it's available for use.
Integrated circuit (IC)	A complex electronic circuit with multiple transistors and other electrical components on a single piece of material.
Keyboard	The easiest and most widely used device for data input.
Kilobyte (K)	1,024 bytes and usually abbreviated simply as K, for example 512K.
Laser printer	Printer which creates characters on paper with a special printing process involving an industrial laser. Laser printers are still expensive, however they're extremely quiet and create very good print quality.
Megabyte (Mb)	1,024K and usually abbreviated simply as Mb, for example, 20Mb.
Megahertz (MHz)	A unit of measure which equals a frequency of 1 million cycles per second.
Micro processor	Another word for chip. When used in computer science, the term chip usually refers to the main microprocessor of the computer, which controls the basic functions.

195

Modem   Short for MODulator/DEModulator. This device converts Amiga
                     signals into electrical impulses and transmits these impulses over
                     telephone lines, and converts received impulses back into signals
                     understandable by the Amiga.

Motherboard   Also called logic board. It's the large printed circuit board containing
                     the CPU, support chips, RAM and expansion slots.

Mouse   The easiest and quickest means of cursor control for the Amiga. The
                     mouse is a small box with two buttons on top and a ball poking out
                     the bottom. Moving the mouse on a table moves the cursor in the
                     same direction on the screen.

Multitasking   This is the name given to the Amiga's ability to simultaneously
                     perform several tasks.

Operating   A computer has to know certain facts automatically. If the Amiga starts
system   without a diskette inserted, the system notices this and requests the
                     Workbench diskette. The operating system ensures that the Amiga
                     performs its initial tasks and checks for keyboard or mouse input.

Parallel   Centronics interface, usually leading to a printer (see also *Centronics*).
interface   Parallel interfaces exchange data 8 bits at a time.

Path   Indicates the route the Amiga follows to find a specific file.

Peripheral   All external units connected to the Amiga. External disk drives,
                     printers, modems, etc., are peripherals.

Pixel   Pixels are the individual dots on the screen. Coordinate (0,0) of the
                     Amiga screen represents one pixel. The more pixels a computer can
                     display, the better the *resolution*. The resolution defines the maximum
                     number of dots into which a screen is divided. The picture quality
                     improves and becomes more reliable with higher resolutions.

Printer   Printers transmit data to paper. The Amiga accepts a wide range of
                     printers. Two types of printers are most common: dot-matrix printers
                     and daisywheel printers. Dot-matrix printers are capable of printing
                     graphics. Daisywheel printers cannot print graphics. The main
                     advantage, until recently, of a daisywheel printer was its ability to
                     produce letter quality type. A daisywheel printer is basically a
                     typewriter connected to a computer. Manufacturers have recently
                     produced printers that can print Near Letter Quality (NLQ).

RAM disk   Pseudo disk drive created in the RAM of the Amiga. Because it is not a
                     mechanical device, the RAM disk allows very fast file access, but loses
                     all data when you switch off the Amiga.

                     Amiga users with only one disk drive will find the RAM disk
                     extremely important. Anything can be kept in a RAM disk, provided
                     that the files do not overstep the memory bounds set for the RAM disk.

Random Access Memory (RAM)	RAM is the free memory of the computer. This is memory in which you can store temporarily data. This memory can be read from and written to but is lost when you switch off your Amiga. See also *ROM*.
Read	The process of retrieving data, usually from a disk drive.
Read Only Memory (ROM)	ROM consists of information permanently planted on a chip (see *Chip*), which remains intact after the computer is switched on. When the user switched the computer on, the computer reads the information from this ROM as needed. Unlike RAM, the user cannot write to ROM (hence the name).
Resolution	A measurement expressed in horizontal and vertical dots for printers and pixels for monitors. The larger the resolution the sharper and better the image.
RS-232 interface	Standard serial interface. Serial transfer involves the transfer of data one bit at a time.
Shell	An enhanced version of the Command Line Interface (CLI).
Software	Any programs located on diskettes or in other forms.
Source disk	It's the disk which sends data during the backup procedure. When copying data from one disk to another, the disk being copied is the source disk and the destination disk is the disk receiving data.
Subdirectory	Refers to a relative directory stored within another directory.
User interface	The communication point between the user and the computer (such as the keyboard, mouse or joystick).
Utilities	Programs that either help the programmer program more efficiently, or act as tools for helping the user in disk and file management. Some utilities optimize the performance of a hard disk, others help the user recover deleted or destroyed files.
Warm start	Warm starting the Amiga means restarting it without turning it off. Pressing Ctrl <Commodore logo> (or left <Amiga>) right <Amiga> executes a warm start. Note for Amiga 1000 owners: When you perform a warm start, the Amiga 1000 doesn't need your Kickstart diskette—it goes right on to the Workbench phase of startup.
Write protect	Protects disks from accidental formatting or file deletion. You can write protect your Amiga disks by moving the write protect slider. Data can be read from this disk but nothing can be changed on the disk.

C: IconEditor   (2.0)

The icon editor allows you to create outstanding icons for any program. For instance, use an icon of little balls for the lotto program (Chapter 3) instead of the BASIC program icon. Other examples of creating icons could include a camera icon for a videocassette database program or a bar graph icon for a statistical graphics program.

Every time you load, edit and save a program in AmigaBASIC, an icon created before this editing session self-destructs and returns to the normal BASIC program icon. You'll save time and effort by creating a new icon _after_ you finish the editing phases of the program. You also might want to store your favorite icon designs in a separate drawer for later use.

- Double-click the `Tools` drawer icon on the `Extras` disk.

- Double-click the `IconEdit` icon.

In a moment the following window opens:

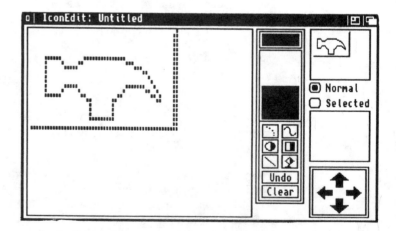

IconEdit Window

The Magnified View Display Box fills most of the `IconEdit` window. To the right of this Box is the Color Selection Gadget. Below this gadget are the gadgets you'll use in creating your icons. The four large arrows allow you to shift your image.

Throughout this book you've seen that the Amiga has a separate information file for each program. Think of all the data displayed in the info window. One important piece of information is the program's source (BASIC, Notepad, etc.). The Amiga stores this information in a file with the same name as the program itself and with an .info suffix. When you create new icons, make sure you use icons of the same or similar type as the new program. Here's an overview of the various icon types:

Type	Example
diskette	Workbench icon
directory	empty drawer
tool	icon ed. icon
project file	notepad project icon

The Magnified View Display Box is the area where you'll actually design the icon. Designing and creating an icon is very similar to designing a pointer (Chapter 2).

- Move the pointer to the Magnified View Display Box.

- Click the left mouse button once.

Note that a dot appears in the window at the location you clicked in the magnified view. This large window is where you edit your pointer.

- Move the mouse to a different location in the window and click the left mouse button again.

- Press and hold the left mouse button, and move the pointer around in the magnified view. Create a circle in the window.

- Release the left mouse button.

Let's change the color of the pointer.

- Move the pointer to one of the four color selection gadgets (don't use the same color as in the previous steps) box just above the RGB sliders and click on it. The box above the four colors will change to the color you selected.

- Move the pointer into the magnified view.

- Press and hold the left mouse button. Move the pointer in a circular motion.

- Release the left mouse button.

The pointer now draws a circle in the new color. Although the circle may appear more jagged in the magnified view, it will appear rounder in the smaller window. The many dots form lines and smoother shapes when you view them in normal size.

- Click on the Clear gadget.

This clears the Magnified View Display Box.

You can select more than one color in the Color Selection Gadget:

- Select the first color.

- Press either ⬆ key and select the additional color(s).

This allows you to create a checkerboard pattern as a fill for circles or boxes.

Notice the six gadgets below the Color Selection Gadgets. These gadgets will help your designs.

- Select the circle gadget (left center gadget). The picture of the small circle will change to indicate it was selected.

- Move the pointer to the Magnified View Display Box.

- Press the left mouse button. Move the cursor down and to the left.

Notice that the size of the circle increases as you move the mouse.

- When the circle is at the desired size, release the left mouse button.

Experiment with the other five design gadgets. These gadgets include:

Freehand gadget allows you to draw free drawings or sketches. This is not a very accurate method because the pointer moves quickly in the window. The lines are not always straight or continuous.

Continuous Freehand gadget is similar to freehand gadget but the pointer moves slower and draws continuous lines. In fact, it may take a second before the design catches up to the movement of the pointer.

We briefly discussed the Circle Gadget above. However, there are additional features available with this gadget. For example, you can double the width of the circle.

- Click on the upper left corner of the circle gadget. Move the pointer to the desired location in the magnified box.

- Press the left mouse button to start the circle and continue moving the mouse until the circle reaches the desired size.

- Before releasing the left mouse button, press and hold the Ctrl key. Then release both at the same time.

You can use a pattern to fill the circle.

- Select the lower right corner of the circle gadget. Move the pointer to the desired location in the magnified box.

- Press the left mouse button to start the circle and continue moving the mouse until the circle reaches the desired size.

- Release the left mouse button to fill the circle.

Select the `Line Gadget` if you want to draw straight lines.

- Select the line gadget and move the pointer to the beginning spot of the line. Press the left mouse button. A small dot will appear at this location.

- Do not release the left mouse button yet. Move the pointer to the end spot of the line. Notice that the line follows the movement of the pointer.

- When the line is at the desired length and angle (make sure it's straight), release the left mouse button.

- You can double the width of the line by pressing the `Ctrl` key before releasing the left mouse button. Then release both at the same time.

Select the `Box Gadget` if you want to draw boxes and rectangles.

- Select the upper left corner for a normal box or select the lower right corner to design a filled box.

- You can double the width of the box by pressing the `Ctrl` key before releasing the left mouse button. Then release both at the same time.

`Fill gadget` allows you to select an area in the window and fill that area with a color.

You can fill in previously empty circles and boxes or change the fill colors of existing circles and boxes. Select the upper left corner for a normal box or select the lower right corner to design a filled box.

If you make a mistake, select the `Undo gadget`. Select this gadget whenever you want to save the design but want to cancel the last mouse action.

IconEdit Menus

Press the right mouse button to display the `IconEdit` menus. A menu bar appears at the top of the screen:

`Project    Type    Highlight    Images    Misc`

Project

This menu lists the items you'll need to save and open various icon files.

Most of the items in this menu are self-explanatory or were explained in previous sections.

The important new item is the **Save As Default Icon**. This item allows you to save the current image in the Magnified View Display Box. The Workbench then uses this display as the default icon when you select `Show All Files` menu item.

Type

You'll select the items in this menu to specify the type of icon you're designing. You can select from the following five items:

`Disk` to represent the disk icons appearing in the Workbench window.

`Drawer` to represent the drawer icons appearing in the disk window.

`Tool` to represent a tool. This is the default type.

`Project` to represent an icon which was created by a tool.

`Garbage` to represent the trashcan drawer.

HiLite

While using the Amiga, you've probably noticed that the appearance of different parts of an icon may change when the icon is selected. This menu contains three items that enable you to control the appearance of the selected icon.

`Complement` highlights the entire icon.

`Backfill` highlights the icon and not the background of the box.

`Image` creates a new or different appearance for the icon. For example, the drawer icon does not change color when it is selected but a new image of an open drawer appears to show it's selected.

Images

`Exchange` switches between images of the Normal mode and the Selected mode.

If you select the normal view, `Copy` copies the image in the normal view to the selected view.

If you select the selected view, `Copy` copies the image in the selected view to the normal view.

`Load` loads previously saved images. You can load `Normal Image` to load the normal (unselected) image of the icon you selected or `Selected Image` to load the selected image of the icon you specified.

`Both Images` loads selected and normal images of the icon you specified in the corresponding boxes.

`IFF Brush` loads an IFF (Interchange File Format) file from another program. The location where this file is loaded depends on if you selected Normal or Selected.

`Save IFF Brush` saves your image in the IFF format.

`Restore` returns the original icon display (the one displayed when you first opened the window).

Misc   `Grid` magnifies each pixel in the display.

`Remap B/W` switches the display between a white/black background and a white/black foreground.

`Auto Top Left` automatically moves the display to the upper left corner of the magnified view box.

D: IconEditor (1.3)

The icon editor allows you to create outstanding icons for any program.
For instance, in the lotto program, you could make an icon of little
balls instead of the usual BASIC program icon. A videocassette
database program could have a camera icon or a statistical graphics
program could have a bar graph icon.

Every time you load, edit and save a program in AmigaBASIC, an icon
created before this editing session self-destructs and returns to the
normal BASIC program icon. You'll save time and effort by creating a
new icon <u>after</u> you finish the editing phases of the program. You also
might want to store your favorite icon designs in a separate drawer for
later use.

*   Double-click the Tool drawer icon on the Extras disk.

*   Double-click the IconEd icon.

Once the editor loads, a large white window appears. This window
contains general data about the available icon types. Throughout this
book you've seen that the Amiga has a separate information file for
each program. Think of all the data displayed in the info window. One
important piece of information is the program's source (BASIC,
Notepad, etc.). The Amiga stores this information in a file with the
same name as the program itself and with an .info suffix. When you
create new icons, make sure you use icons of the same or similar type
as the new program. Here's an overview of the various icon types:

Type	Example
diskette	Workbench icon
directory	empty drawer
tool	icon ed. icon
project file	notepad project icon

*   Click on the OK gadget.

Now the icon editor displays the editor icon itself, in a large frame (the
Editor window) and in nine smaller frames. The small frames could
each contain different icons, since the icon editor lets you process up to
nine icons at once.

Before you load and change an icon, you must specify the frame of the
icon you want changed.

*   Click on the third frame of the top row.

This frame turns black, indicating that this frame is active.

- Click on the top left small frame.

- Press and hold the right mouse button.

A menu bar appears at the top of the screen:

Color Copy Move Text Disk Misc HiLite

- Move the pointer to the **Disk** menu title, and select the Load Data item.

Now a black requester appears. A string gadget below the heading Load Icon Image Data lets you type in the name of the icon you want loaded.

- Click on the string gadget.

- Use the [Backspace] key to erase unwanted text to the left of the cursor and the [Del] key to erase everything to the right of the cursor.

- Enter:

    df0:trashcan

- Click the Load Icon Image gadget.

The Trashcan icon appears in the large frame and the upper left small frame.

You already know from the section on AmigaDOS that the Amiga has subdirectories. If, for example, you wish to load a program called Dialog from the BASICDemos drawer (subdirectory), then you must also specify this:

    df0:BASICDemos/Dialog

You must also always specify the disk drive. It is essential that you already know the name of the icon you wish to change, because the editor has no DIR or LIST command available.

Whenever you wish to load other icons, you must activate a new frame into which the icon goes. Anything else in this frame erases.

Color

The **Color** pulldown menu enables you to specify the color in which you wish to draw. Select the color you want. The active color has a checkmark to the left of the color bar.

Copy

This menu moves icons between icon frames. The Undo Frame item cancels all changes made to an icon, provided the original icon is still on diskette. The Snapshot Frame item stores the image currently in the **Editor** window. Selecting Undo Frame restores the original icon.

- Select the Snapshot Frame item from the **Copy** pulldown menu.

From Frame relocates an icon from one frame into the active frame. The window from which the copy comes is indicated by a set of number options.

- Move the pointer onto the From Frame item of the **Copy** pulldown menu (do not release the right mouse button).

A set of number options appears, numbered 1 to 9.

- Move the pointer onto the option number 4 and release the right mouse button.

The Trashcan icon disappears. From Frame transfers the old icon to the **Editor** window, and erases the old icon from its original frame. However, you clicked Snapshot Frame earlier, so you can easily restore the Trashcan icon.

- Select the Undo Frame item from the **Copy** pulldown menu.

You can also copy the Trashcan icon using this method:

- Click the upper right frame.

- Press and hold the right mouse button and move the pointer onto the **Copy** pulldown menu.

- Move the pointer onto the From Frame item.

- Move the pointer onto option number 1 and release the right mouse button.

You now have a duplicate of the Trashcan icon.

The Merge With Frame item lets you merge two icons in one frame.

- Select 2 from the Merge With Frame item.

This displays the icon editor icon on top of the Trashcan. However, the colors have changed. The Trashcan remains almost the same except that part of its black line has disappeared. However, the icon editor is a completely different color. The reason is that certain color conditions apply to the editor. The following explanation assumes that your Amiga system uses the default Workbench colors:

When blue overlaps any other color, the other color appears instead. When orange overlaps white or black, orange appears.

Keep these color combinations in mind when merging different icon frames.

You can now perform one of the basic items of the editor, drawing with the mouse cursor, just as you learned with the `Pointer Editing` window in `Preferences` (see Section 2.10).

• Drag the pointer into the `Editor` window field.

• Press and hold the left mouse button and move the mouse.

This draws lines in the `Editor` window. The lines here are finer, which lets you create higher quality graphics.

• Select another color from the `Color` pulldown menu.

• Move the pointer into the `Editor` window again.

• Press and hold the left mouse button and move the pointer around.

This line appears in the selected color.

• Select the `Undo Frame` item from the `Copy` pulldown menu to display the original Trashcan icon.

Move

The `Move` pulldown menu has two items. The `In-Frame` item moves icons within the `Editor` window.

• Select the `In-Frame` item from the `Move` pulldown menu.

A black requester named `Move Image In-Frame` appears. This requester contains four arrow gadgets (up, down, right and left) and a blank box in the center of these arrows. The icon moves in the direction of the arrow you click. If you click the up arrow gadget, the icon moves up, and so on. The box in the center of the arrow gadgets restores the icon to its original position in the `Editor` window.

This requester defaults to the `Single` gadget, which moves the icon in single steps. If you click on the `Repeat` gadget, the icon moves in the direction selected for as long as you hold the left mouse button. Click on the `OK` gadget to accept the new icon position, or the `Cancel` gadget to exit this requester and return the icon to its original position.

• Click on the `Cancel` gadget.

The Exchange With Frame item exchanges the active icon frame with the icon frame selected from the numbered option.

Text

This menu lets you enter text on the icon. Do not confuse the text on the icon with the name below it; the Amiga assigns this program name to the icon. The **Text** menu has just one item, Write Into Frame.

•   Select the Write Into Frame item from the **Text** pulldown menu.

You can enter any text into this string gadget.

•   Click the Text string gadget and enter text.

The Amiga limits you to the amount of text you can enter. The screen flashes if the text is too long.

The Foreground gadget specifies the text color, and the Background gadget specifies the background color.

•   Click the Foreground gadget until you see a Workbench color you like.

•   Click the Background gadget until you see a Workbench color you like.

The Font gadget specifies the font size. There are only two options: TOPAZ_SIXTY and TOPAZ_EIGHTY.

The Mode gadget offers four types of text display. JAM 1 displays the text directly on the icon (i.e., in the foreground color). JAM 2 displays the text in the selected background color. COMPLEMENT displays the exact complement of the background color for the text. In this example, a blue text appears on an orange background. However, if there is a black dot within the orange area, the text there appears in white. INVERSE reverses the colors and interchanges the text and background colors.

The Position gadget specifies the location of the text. When you click on Position, the requester displayed is almost the same as the requester from the In-Frame item of the **Move** pulldown menu.

•   Click on the Position gadget.

•   Look at the requester and click on its Cancel gadget.

The Reset gadget resets the text window to its initial values. The Cancel gadget stops the process without changing the icon text and the OK gadget accepts all the changes in the **Editor** window.

Disk

The `Disk` pulldown menu has items for saving and loading data. When you select the `Save Data` item, the `Save Icon Image Data` requester displays the last icon name used.

Misc

This menu title is the abbreviation for `Miscellaneous`. The `Clear This Frame` item erases the contents of the **Editor** window. The `Flood Fill` item fills in enclosed areas.

• Select the `Flood Fill` item from the **Misc** pulldown menu.

This displays `Flood Fill Activated` in the title bar. If you now click within an area such as the `Trashcan` icon's lid, the entire area fills with the selected color. Remember to select the color before performing this operation.

• Click within the `Trashcan` icon's lid.

`Flood Fill` deactivates immediately after use.

The `Set Bottom Border` item sets the spacing between the bottom of the icon and the icon's program name. The option offers `0` (no space) or `1` (one space).

HiLite

This last menu title specifies whether the icon should appear in `Inverse` (black becomes white, etc.) or `Backfill` (different background color).

• Select the `Save Data` item from the **Disk** pulldown menu.

A requester containing a string gadget and three other gadgets appears.

The string gadget accepts filename input. This gadget retains the last icon name used for loading data or saving data. The ⌜Backspace⌝ and ⌜Del⌝ keys erase text.

The `Save` gadget saves the icon to diskette. The `Cancel` gadget exits the requester without saving the icon data.

The `Frame and Save` gadget allows you to select the size of the area around your icon before saving.

• Click the `Frame and Save` gadget.

• Click in the upper left corner of the **Editor** window icon.

• Move the mouse down and to the right of the icon.

A rectangular frame moves with the pointer.

• Surround the icon with the frame and press the left mouse button.

The Amiga saves the icon you have designed.

E: Technical Data

Processor   Motorola MC 68000 with a clock speed of 7.16 MHz.

User RAM   512 kilobytes available, internally expandable to 1 megabyte, externally expandable to 8 megabytes (Amiga 1000: 256 kilobytes available, expandable to 512 kilobytes).

System ROM   256 kilobytes of ROM, containing startup data (Amiga 1000 uses the Kickstart diskette instead of system ROM).

Mass storage   Built-in floppy disk drive, uses 3.5" double-sided, double density floppy diskettes, with a capacity of about 900 kilobytes per diskette. External floppy disk drives are available.

Interfaces.

Serial keyboard connector with coiled cable (Amiga 1000 only).

RS-232 (serial) interface for connection to a modem, etc.

Centronics (parallel) interface for connection to printers.

Dual joystick/mouse/paddle jacks.

Two audio outputs for connection to a stereo system.

RGB for connection to an RGB monitor.

MONO for connecting to monochrome monitor.

Graphics   Video display modes:

320x200 pixels with 32 possible colors, using a scan frequency of 60 Hz (interlaced). Two colors displayed require about 10 kilobytes of memory. 32 colors require 50 kilobytes.

320x400 pixels with 32 possible colors, using a scan frequency of 30 Hz (interlaced). Two colors displayed require about 20 kilobytes of memory. 32 colors require 100 kilobytes.

640x200 pixels with 16 possible colors, using a scan frequency of 60 Hz. Two colors displayed require about 20 kilobytes of memory. 16 colors require 80 kilobytes.

640x400 pixels with 16 possible colors, using a scan frequency of 320 Hz (interlaced). Two colors displayed require about 40 kilobytes of memory. 16 colors require 160 kilobytes.

There are a possible 4096 colors available on the palette. The graphic processor can have all 4096 colors on the screen in hold and modify mode (HAM), but your screen design is limited in this mode.

The processor can build two different screen displays simultaneously with 8 different colors (not to be confused with window colors).

In addition, 8 sprites can be simultaneously displayed, with a 16 pixel horizontal resolution and an unlimited vertical resolution. The graphic processor (blitter) can use any part of RAM for display memory, and can rapidly transfer other data quickly through the DMA.

Sound

4 channel synthesizer uses a variable waveform with 8-bit resolution at 0 to 7000Hz. Can also generate speech from phonetic interpretation of text.

Index

T-Z

Abacus

Amiga Catalog

Order Toll Free 1-800-451-4319